# ROCK

## CLASSICS

## Partituras para aficionados al piano

MA
NON
TROPPO

©2021, Miguel Ángel Fernández Pérez

©2021, Redbook Ediciones, s. l., Barcelona

Diseño de cubierta: Regina Richling

ISBN: 978-84-18703-06-5

Depósito legal: B-9.477-2021

Impreso por Ingrabar, Industrias Gráficas Barcelona, c/ Perú. 144, 08020 Barcelona

Impreso en España - *Printed in Spain*

# ROCK CLASSICS

## *Partituras para aficionados al piano*

1.- "**LET IT BE**" - *The Beatles* — 5

2.- "**ANGIE**" - *The Rolling Stones* — 8

3.- "**THE SOUND OF SILENCE**" - *Simon & Garfunkel* — 10

4.- "**LOVE ME TENDER**" - *Elvis Presley* — 12

5.- "**THE HOUSE OF THE RISING SUN**" - *The Animals* — 13

6.- "**STARMAN**" - *David Bowie* — 16

7.- "**NOTHING ELSE MATTERS**" - *Metallica* — 18

8.- "**IMAGINE**" - *John Lennon* — 20

9.- "**THE RIVER**" - *Bruce Springsteen* — 22

10.- "**BLOWIN´ IN THE WIND**" - *Bob Dylan* — 26

11.- "**PIANO MAN**" - *Billy Joel* — 27

12.- "**STAIRWAY TO HEAVEN**" - *Led Zeppelin* — 30

13.- "**HOTEL CALIFORNIA**" - *Eagles* — 33

14.- "**DON´T STOP ME NOW**" - *Queen* — 37

15.- "**ANNIE´S SONG**" - *John Denver* — 42

16.- "**HEART OF GOLD**" - *Neil Young* — 44

17.- "**SORRY SEEMS TO BE THE HARDEST WORD**" - *Elton John* — 46

18.- "**EVERY BREATH YOU TAKE**" - *The Police* — 48

19.- "**LAYLA**" - *Eric Clapton* — 52

20.- "**MOONSHADOW**" - *Cat Stevens* — 54

# ROCK CLASSICS

## Partituras para aficionados al piano

21.- "**LOVE**" - *John Lennon*      **58**

22.- "**ROCK ´N´ ROLL RADIO**" - *Ramones*      **62**

23.- "**SMOKE ON THE WATER**" - *Deep Purple*      **64**

24.- "**MAD WORLD**" - *Tears for Fears*      **66**

25.- "**TIME IN A BOTTLE**" - *Jim Croce*      **68**

26.- "**TEARS IN HEAVEN**" - *Eric Clapton*      **70**

27.- "**LIGHT MY FIRE**" - *The Doors*      **74**

28.- "**LIFE ON MARS?**" - *David Bowie*      **78**

29.- "**GOING HOME (THEME FROM LOCAL HERO)**" - *Dire Straits*   **80**

30.- "**SOMETHING**" - *The Beatles*      **83**

31.- "**WITH OR WITHOUT YOU**" - *U2*      **86**

32.- "**BRIDGE OVER TROUBLED WATER**" - *Simon & Garfunkel*   **90**

33.- "**MORNING HAS BROKEN**" - *Cat Stevens*      **94**

34.- "**I GUESS THAT´S WHY THEY CALL IT THE BLUES**" - *Elton John* **97**

35.- "**SUMMER OF ´69**" - *Bryan Adams*      **100**

36.- "**MESSAGE IN A BOTTLE**" - *The Police*      **103**

37.- "**DESPERADO**" - *Eagles*      **107**

38.- "**JUST THE WAY YOU ARE**" - *Billy Joel*      **110**

39.- "**KASHMIR**" - *Led Zeppelin*      **114**

40.- "**BOHEMIAN RHAPSODY**" - *Queen*      **118**

# "Let It Be"
## The Beatles

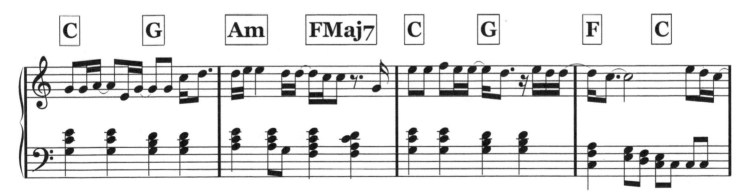

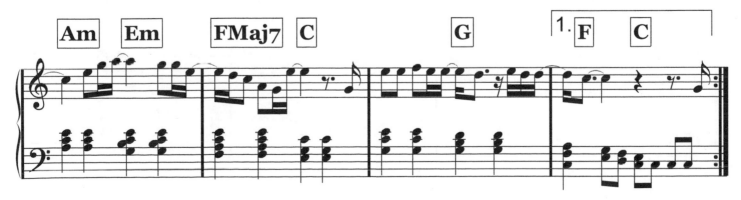

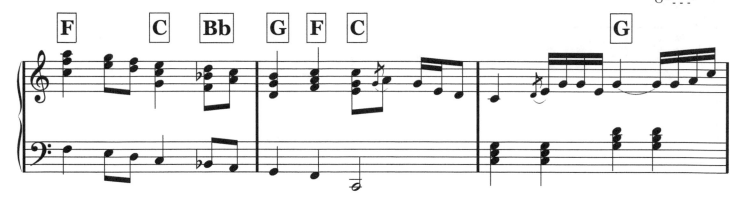

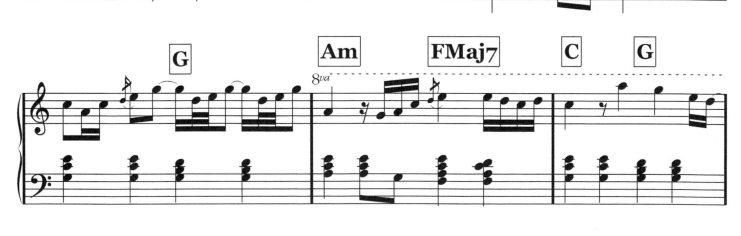

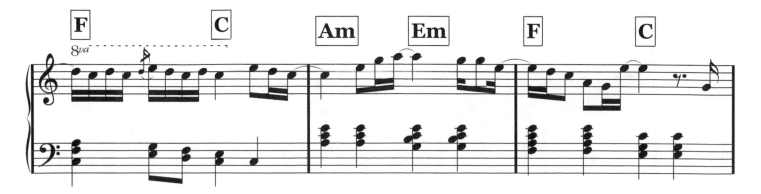

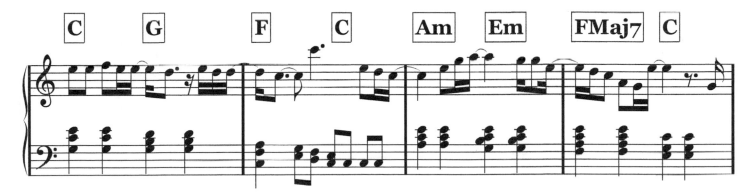

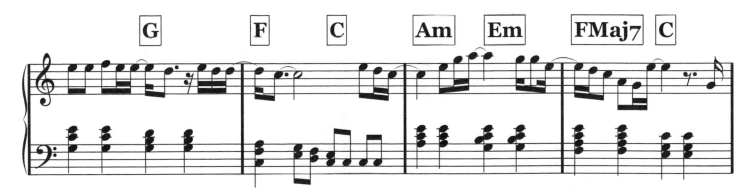

# "Angie"
## The Rolling Stones

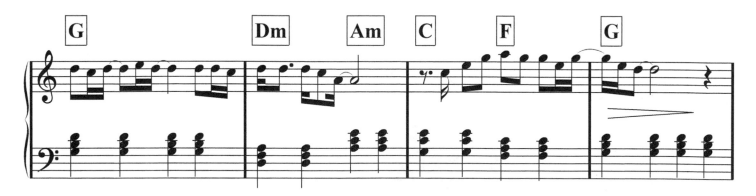

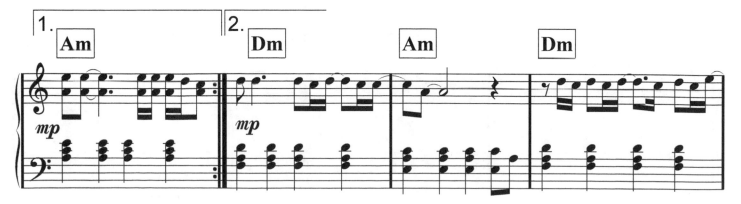

# "The Sound of Silence"
## Simon & Garfunkel

- 11 -

# "Love Me Tender"

## Elvis Presley

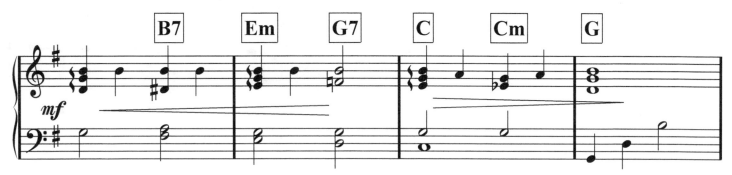

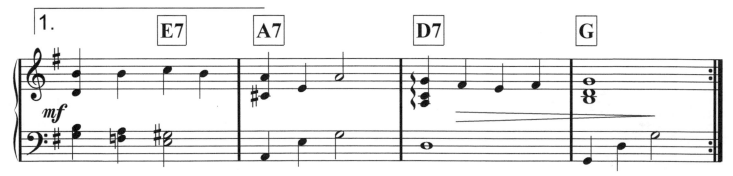

# "The House of the Rising Sun"

## The Animals

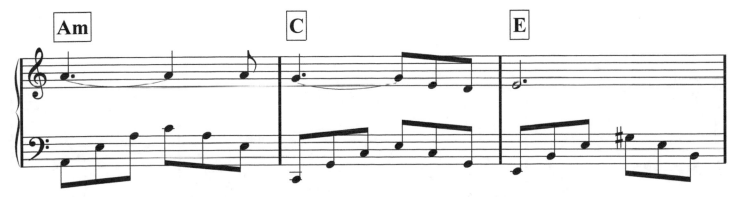

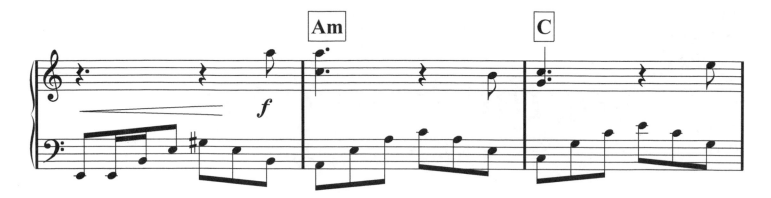

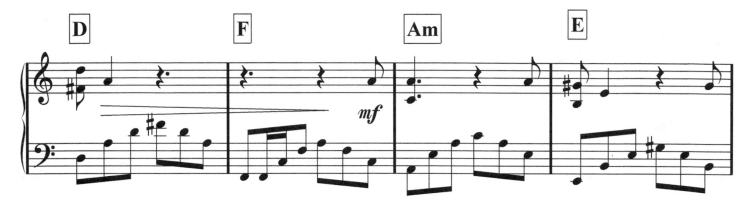

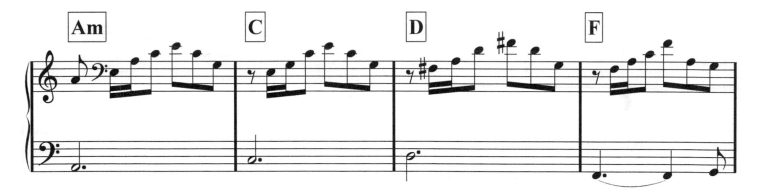

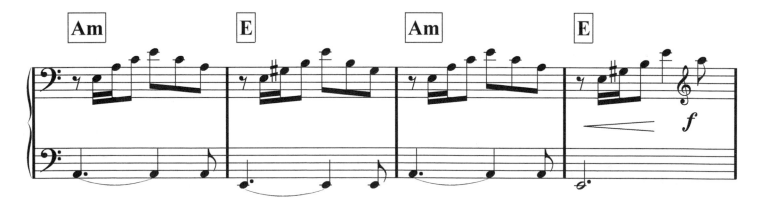

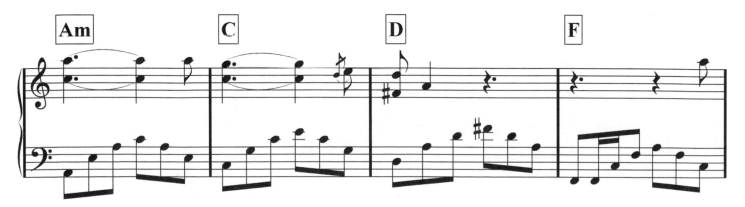

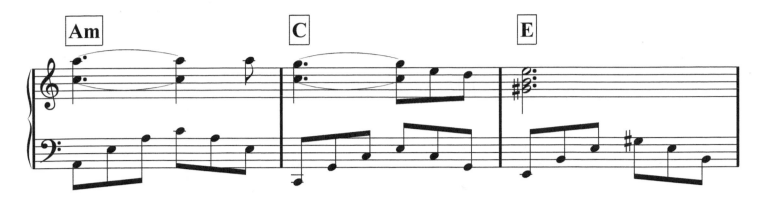

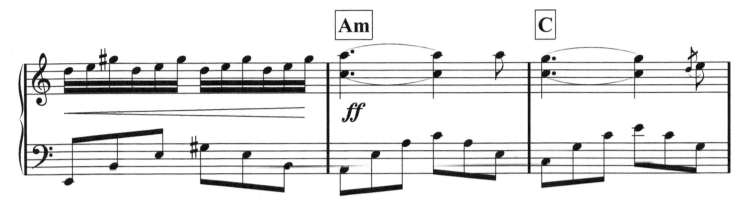

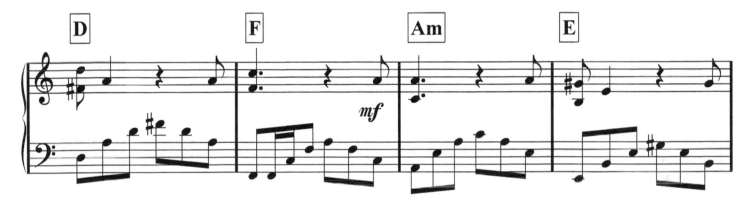

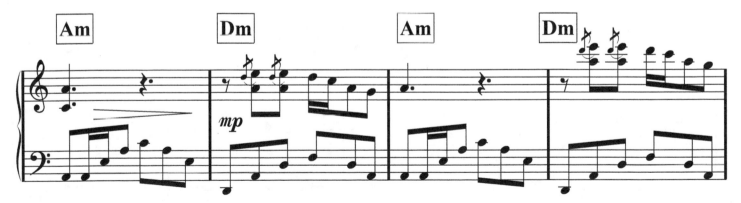

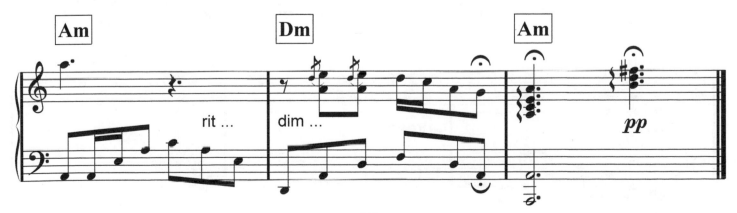

# "Starman"
## David Bowie

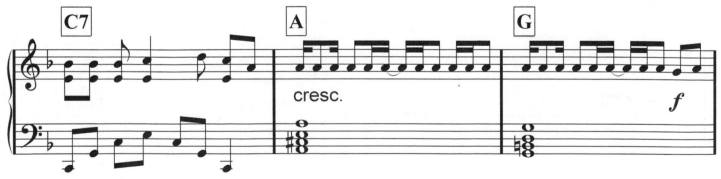

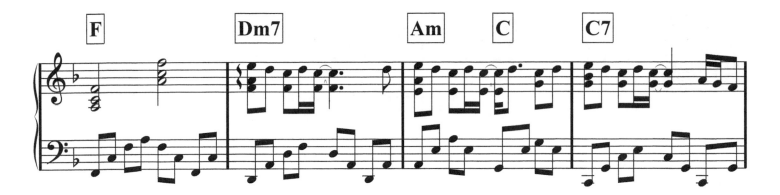

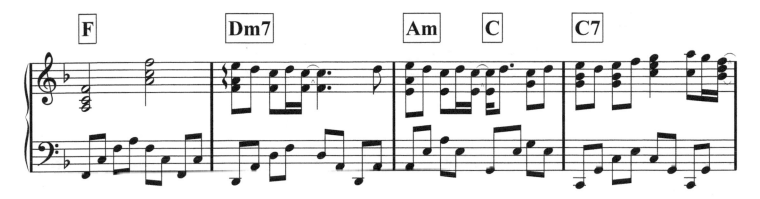

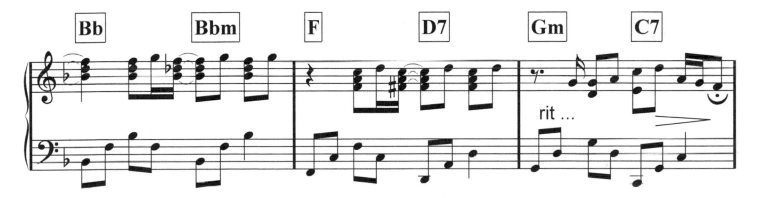

# "Nothing Else Matters"

## *Metallica*

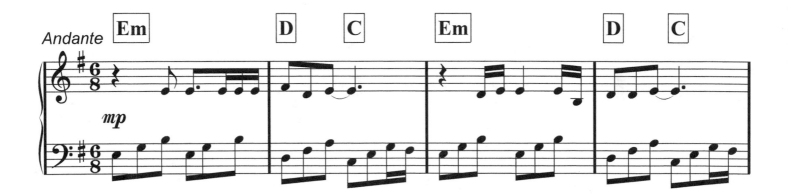

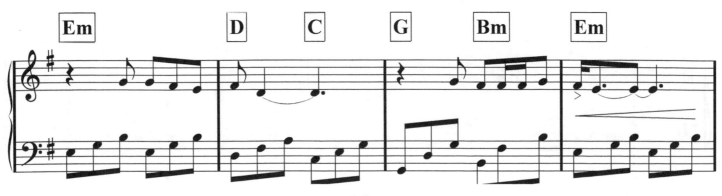

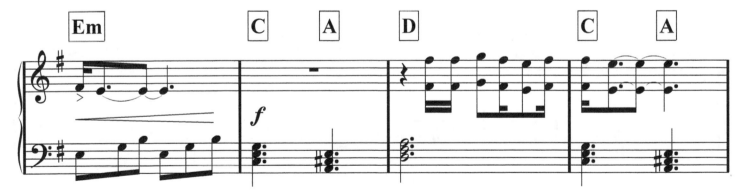

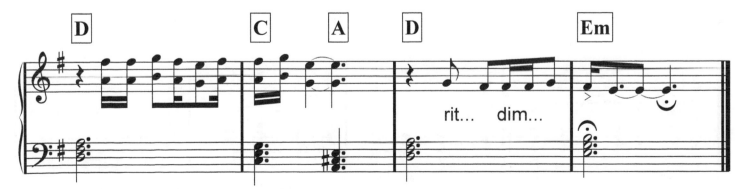

# "Imagine"
## John Lennon

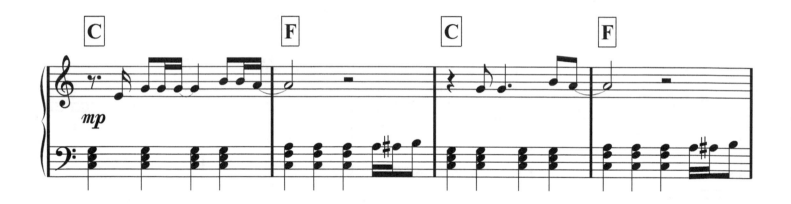

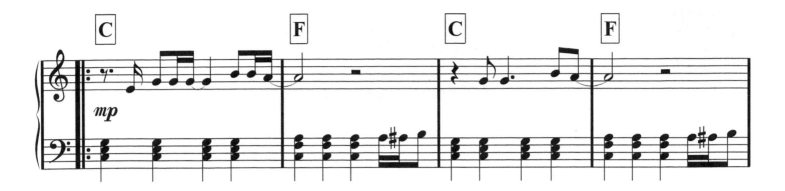

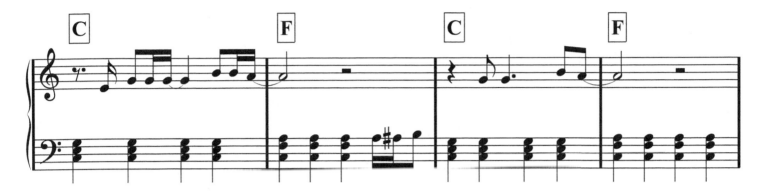

# "The River"
## Bruce Springsteen

# "Blowin´ in the Wind"
## Bob Dylan

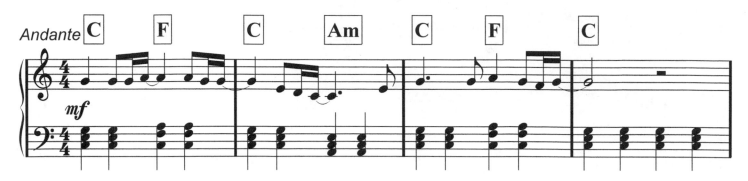

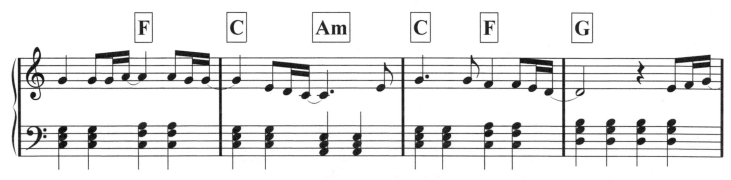

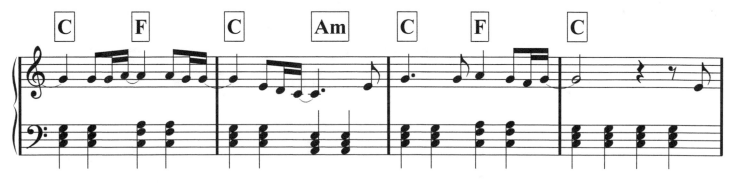

# "Piano Man"
## Billy Joel

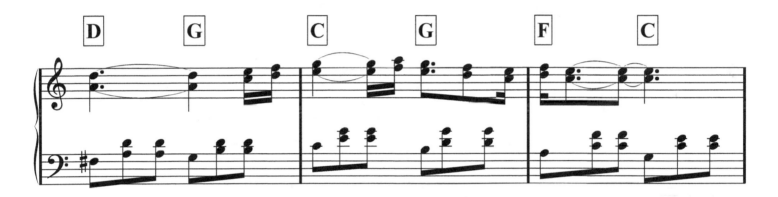

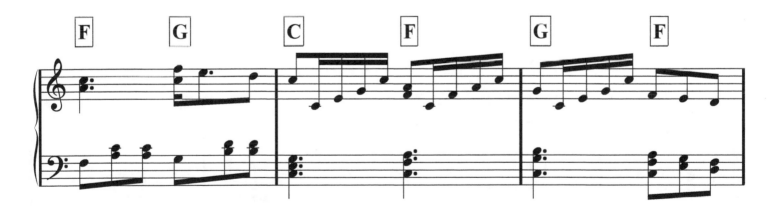

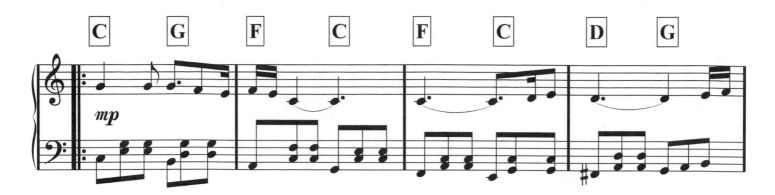

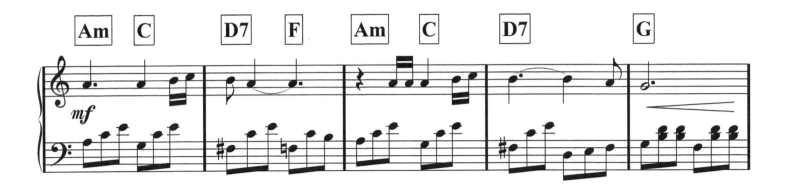

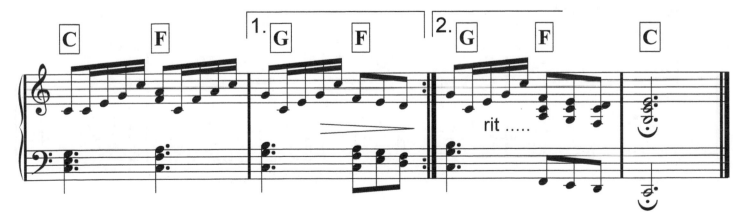

# "Stairway to Heaven"
## Led Zeppelin

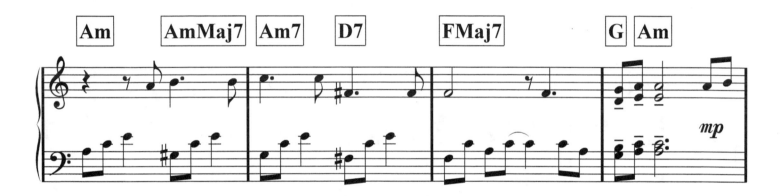

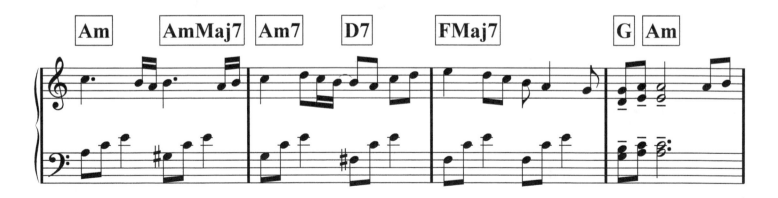

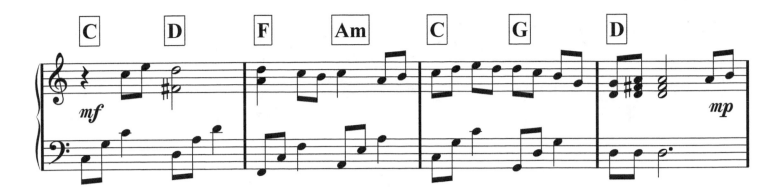

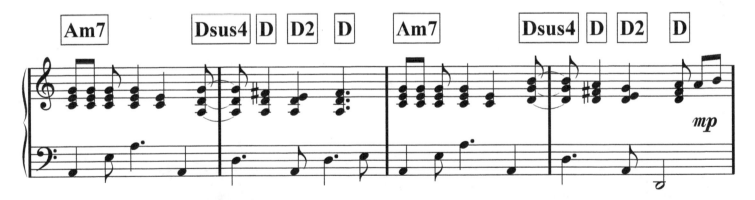

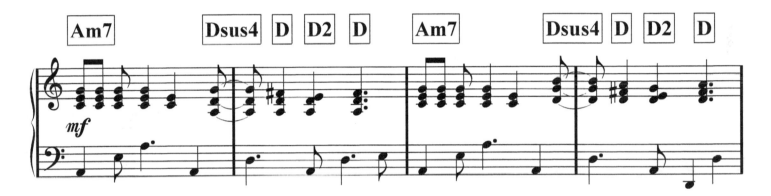

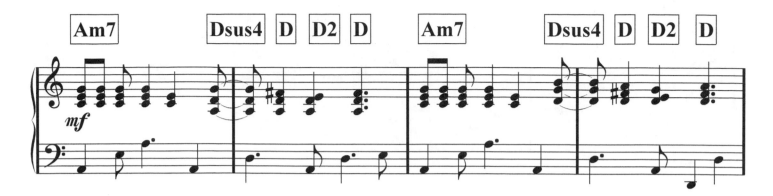

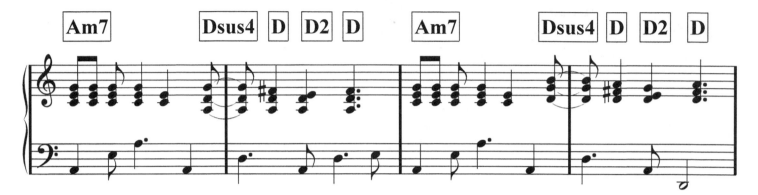

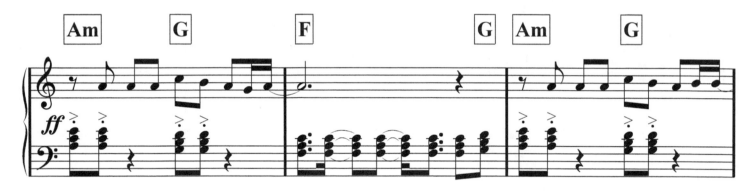

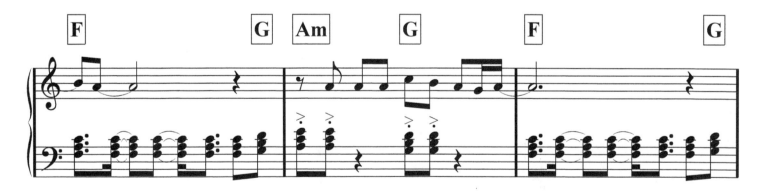

# "Hotel California"
## Eagles

**Bm**     **F#**

*Andante*

**A**     **E**

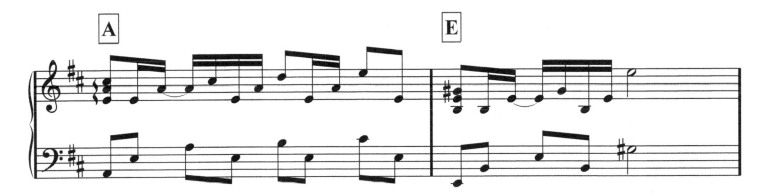

**G**     **D**

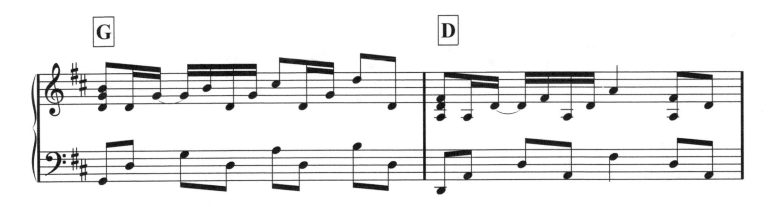

**Em**     **F#**

*rit ...*

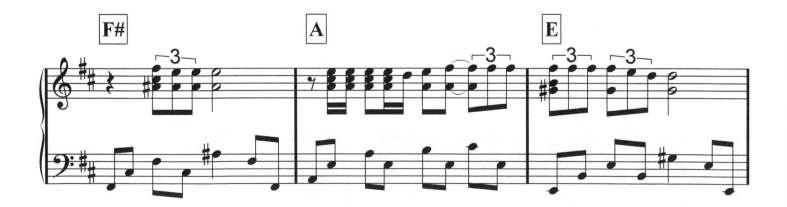

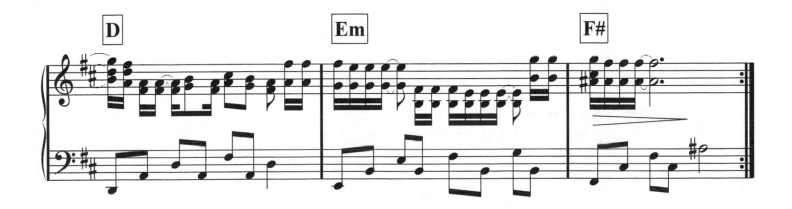

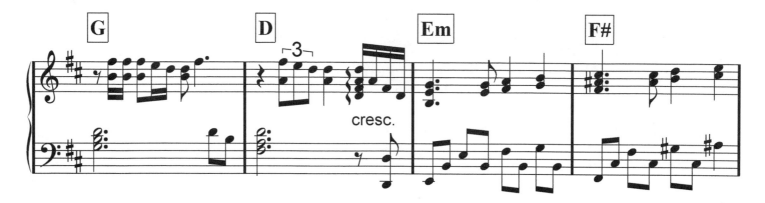

# "Don´t Stop Me Now"
## Queen

accel.... cresc...

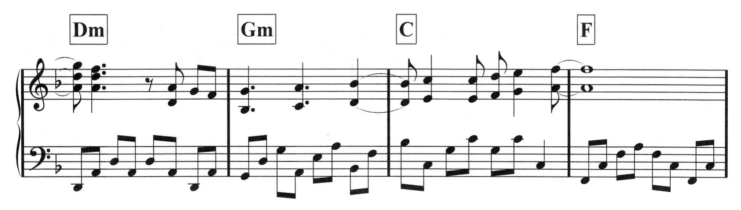

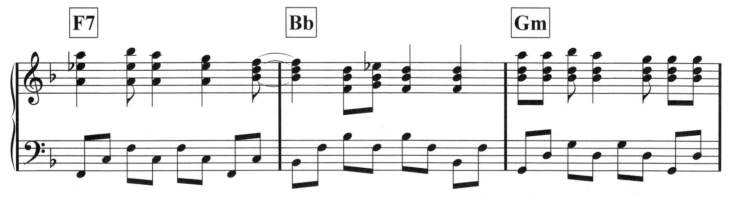

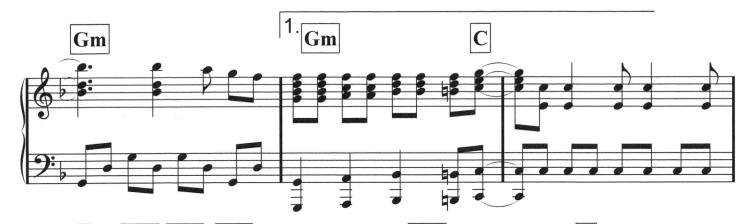

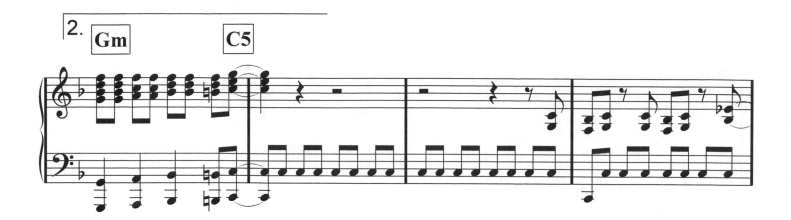

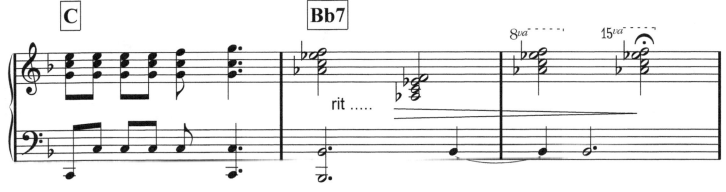

# "Annie´s Song"
## John Denver

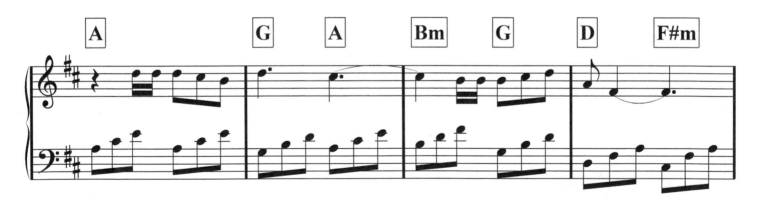

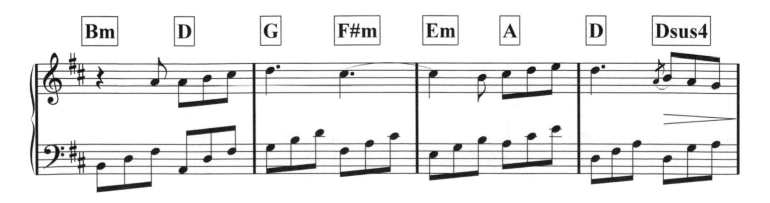

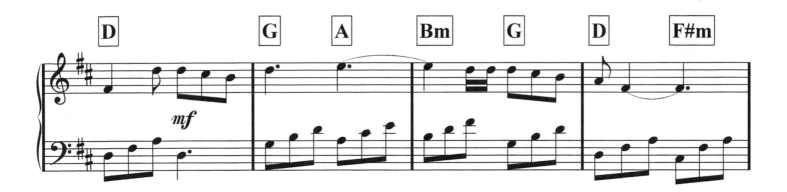

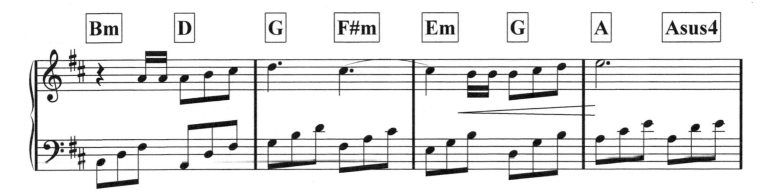

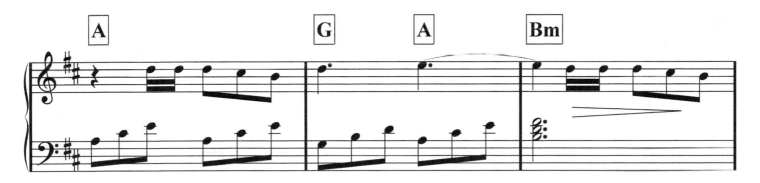

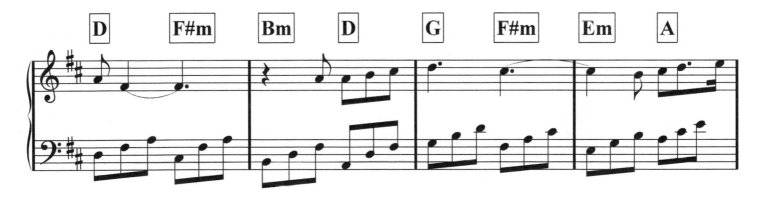

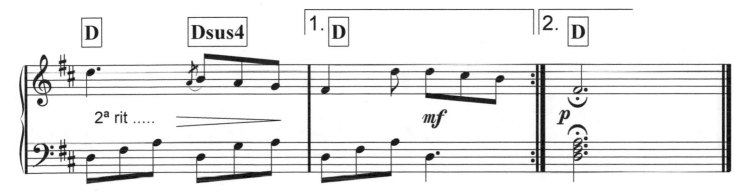

# "Heart of Gold"
## Neil Young

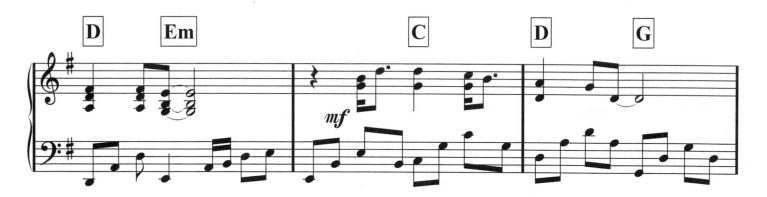

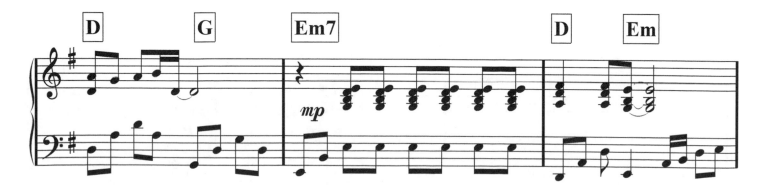

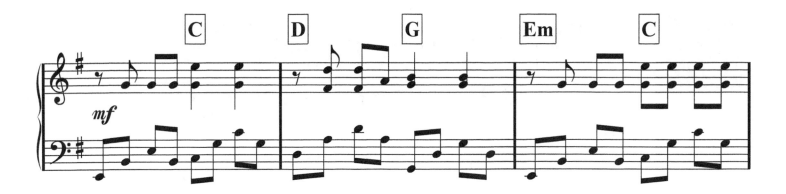

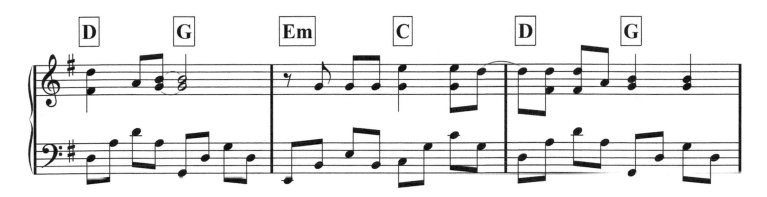

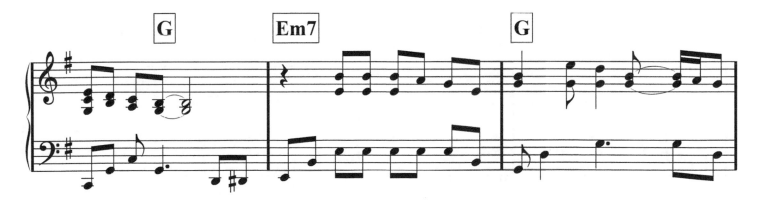

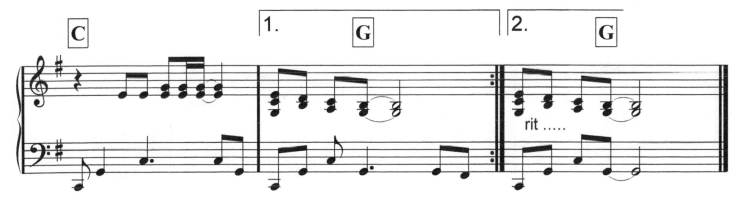

# "Sorry Seems to Be the Hardest Word"

## Elton John

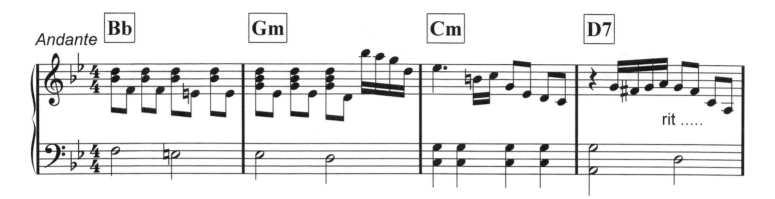

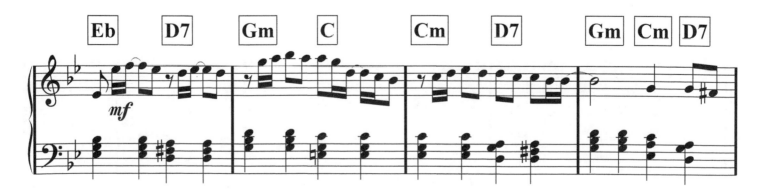

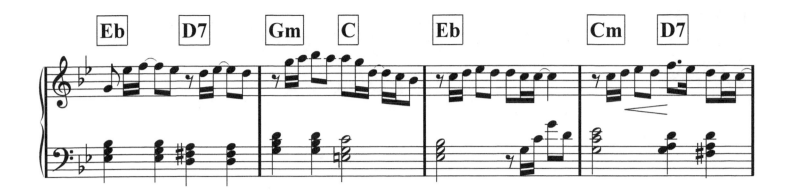

# "Every Breath You Take"
## The Police

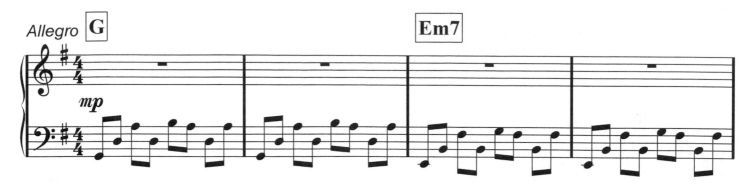

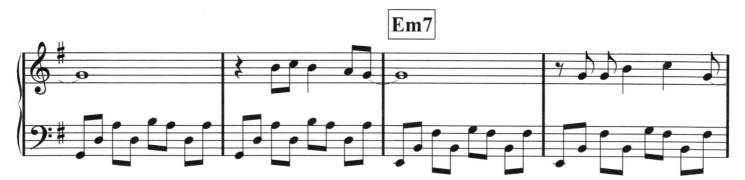

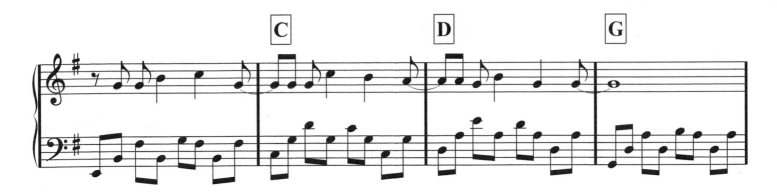

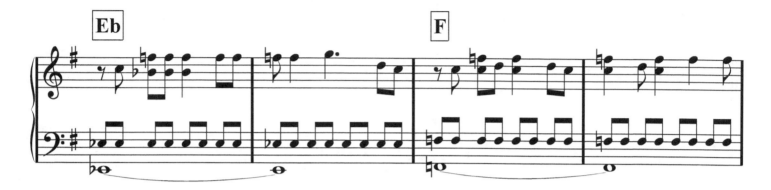

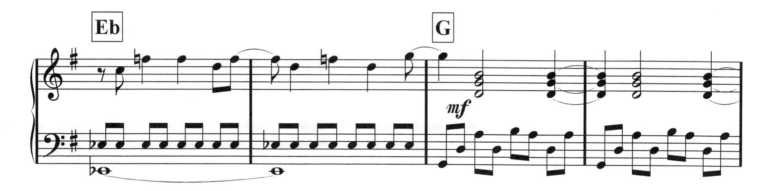

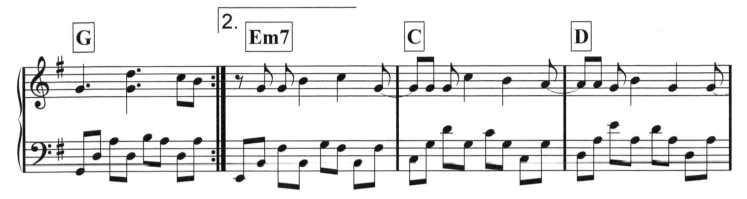

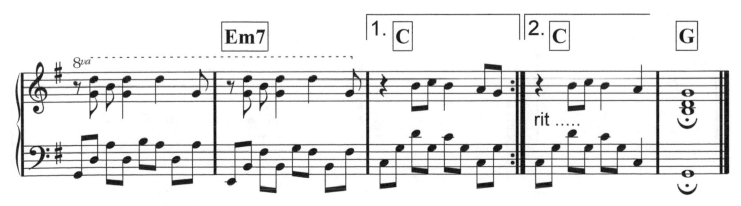

# "Layla"

## Eric Clapton

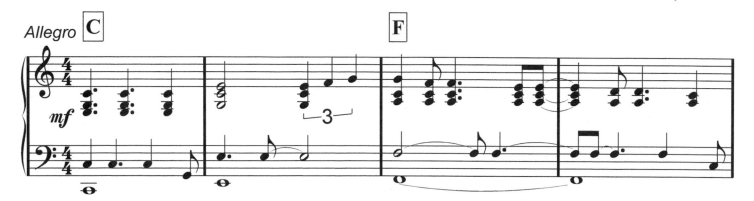

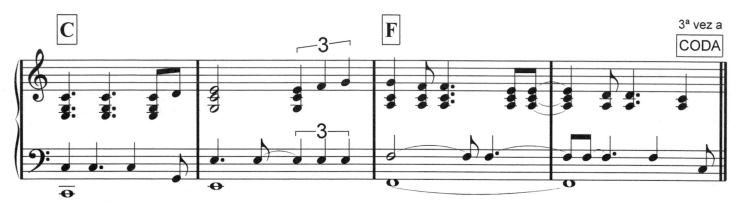

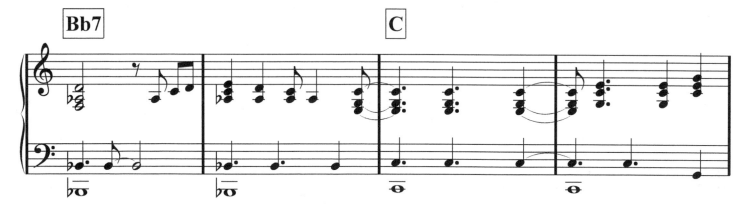

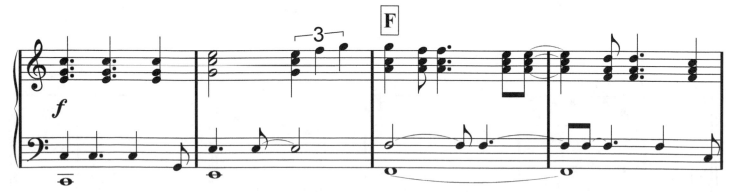

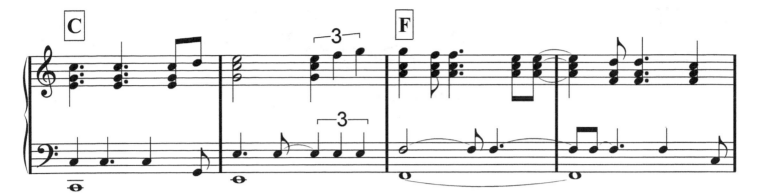

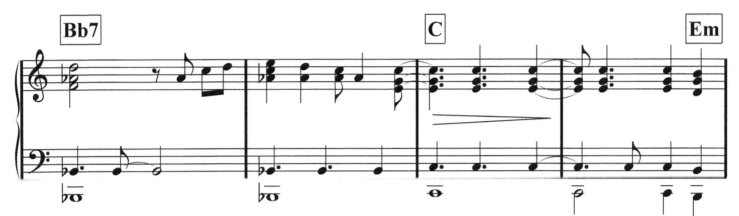

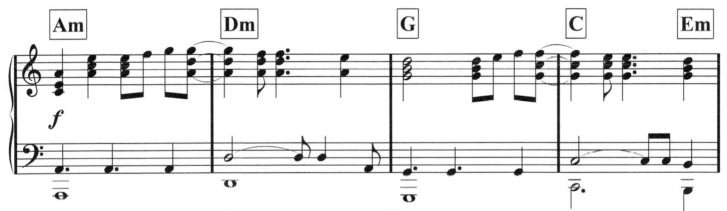

# "Moonshadow"
## Cat Stevens

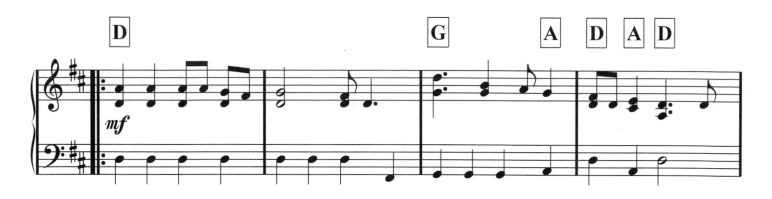

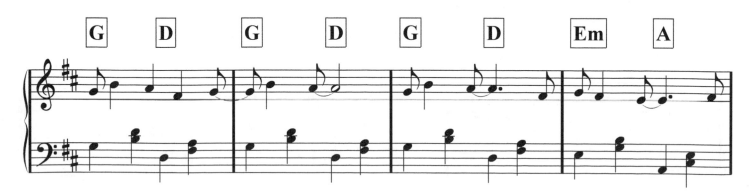

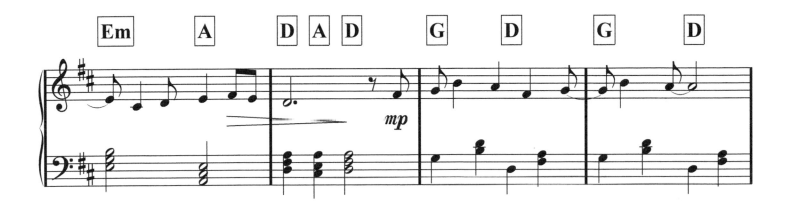

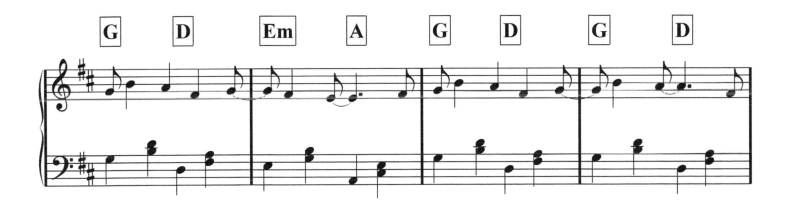

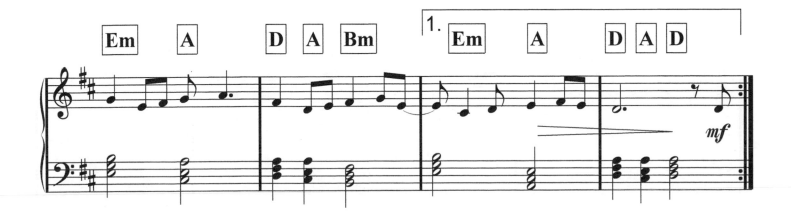

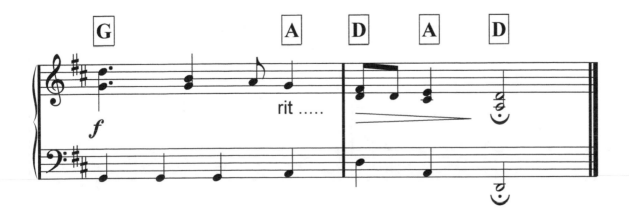

# "Love"
## John Lennon

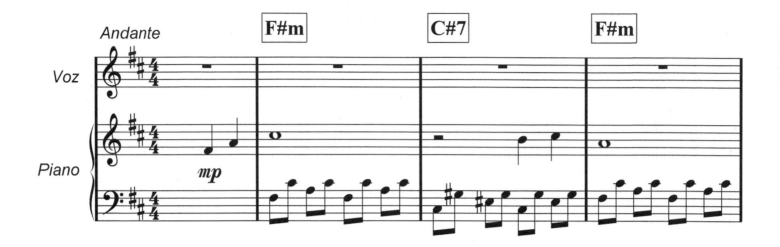

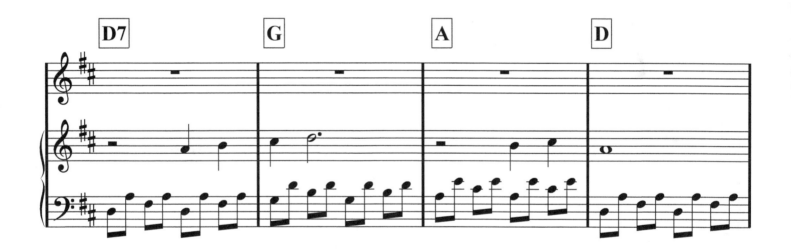

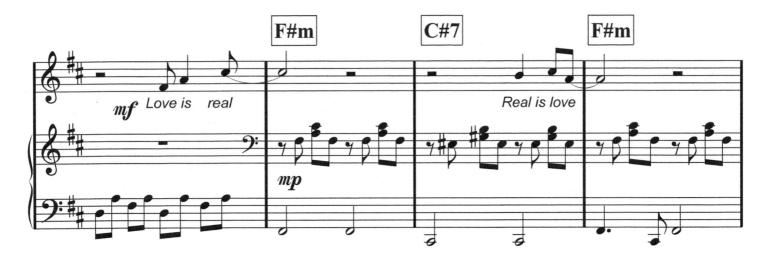

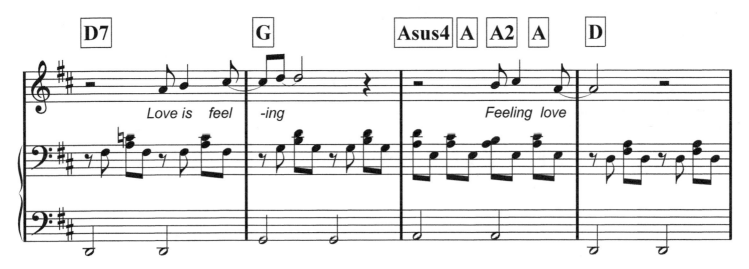

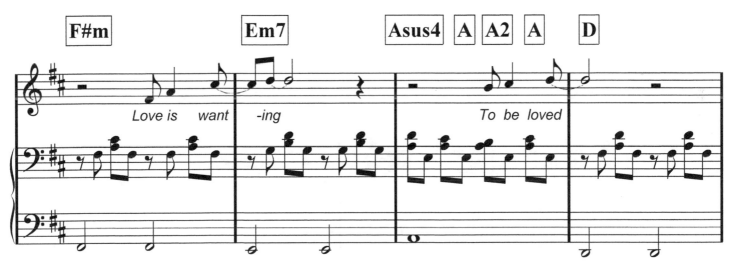

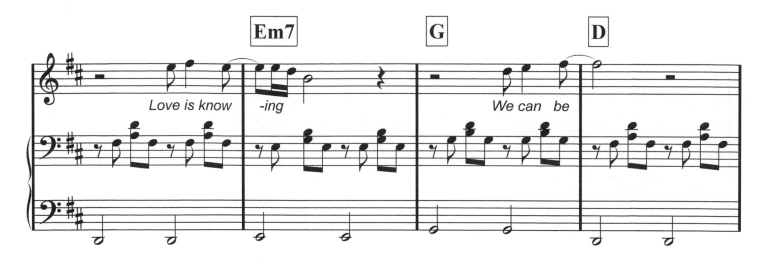

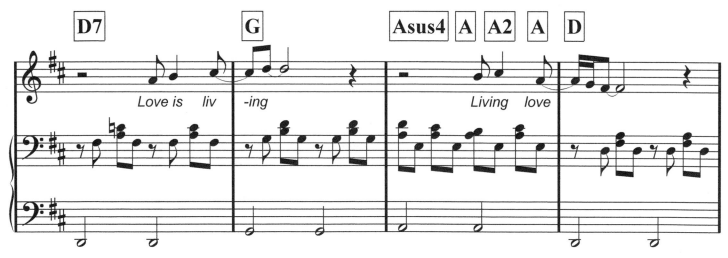

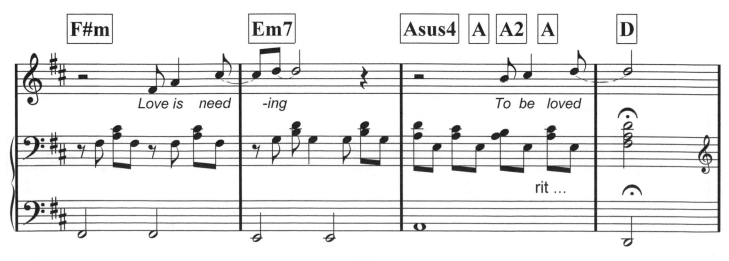

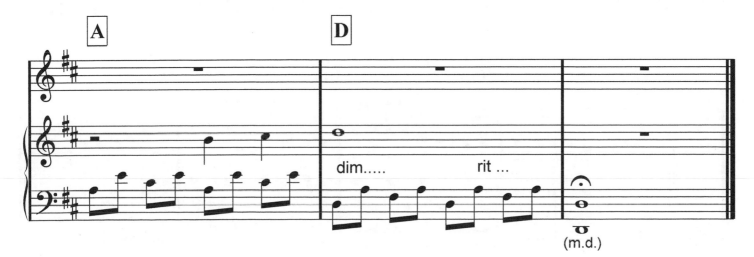

# "Do You Remember
# Rock ´n´Roll Radio?"
## Ramones

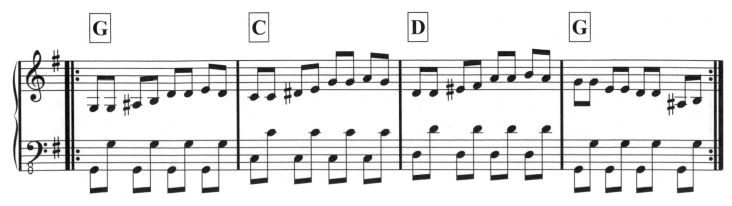

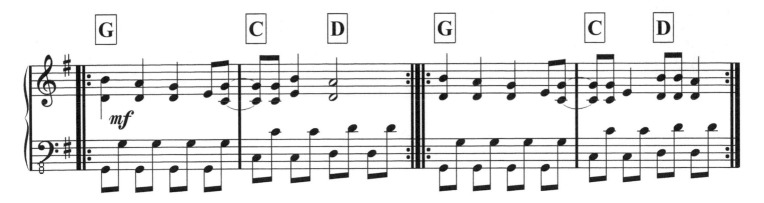

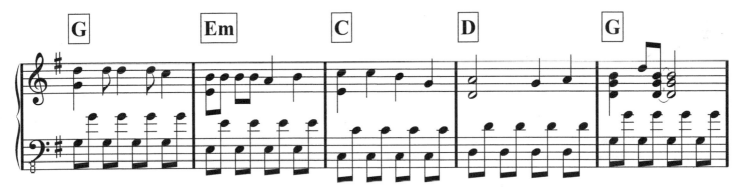

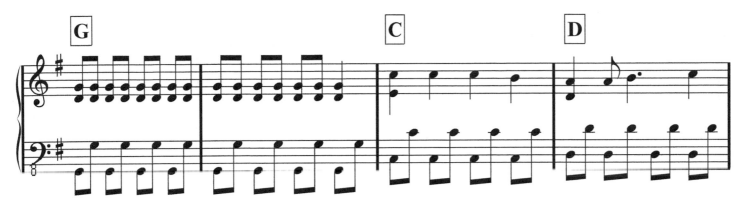

# "Smoke on the Water"
## Deep Purple

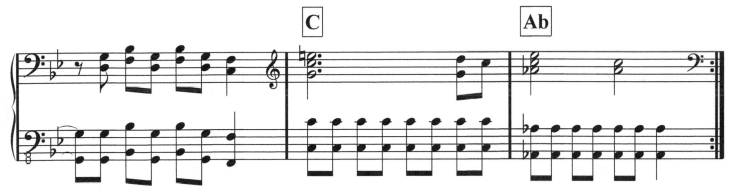

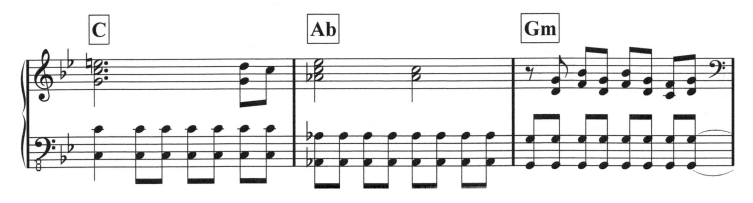

# "Mad World"
## Tears for Fears

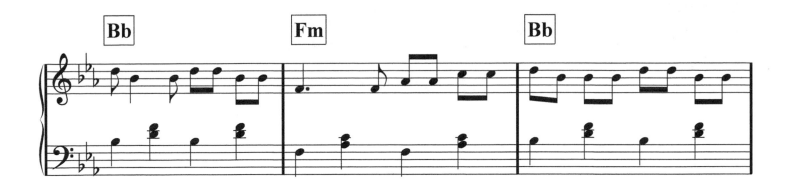

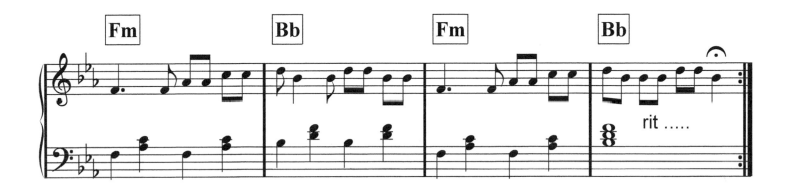

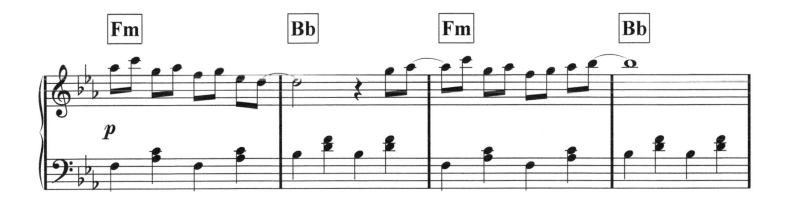

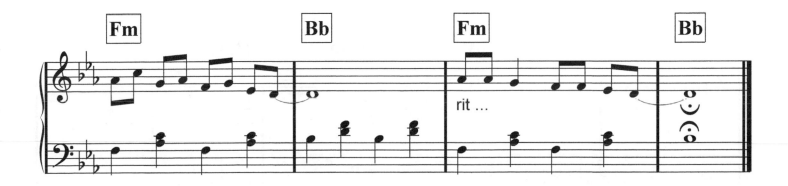

# "Time in a Bottle"

## Jim Croce

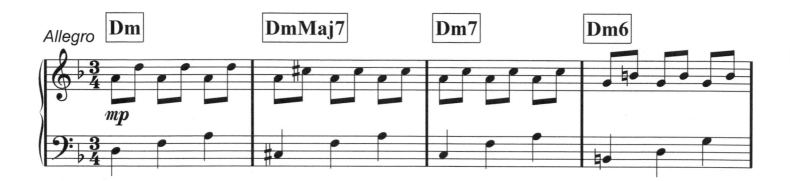

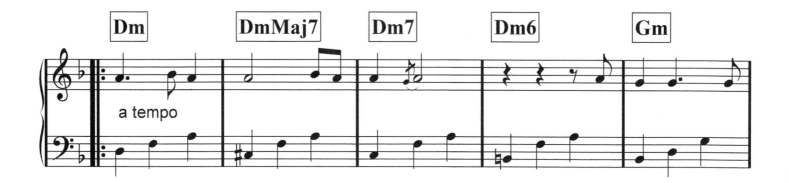

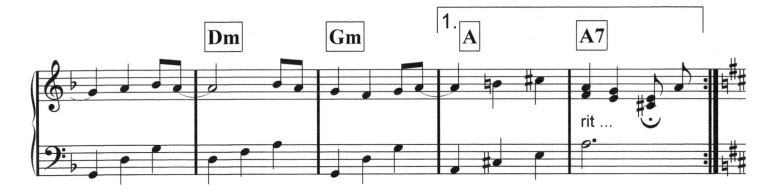

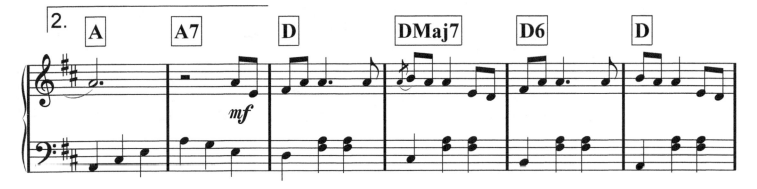

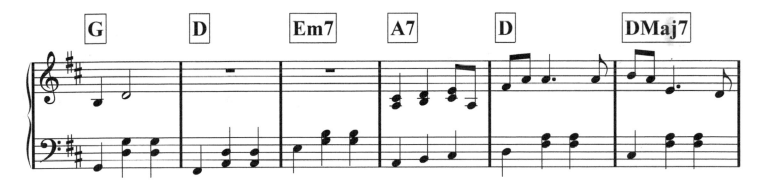

# "Tears in Heaven"
## Eric Clapton

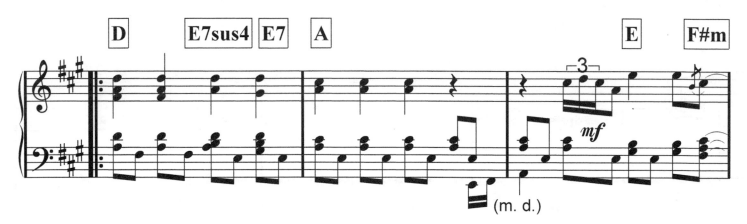

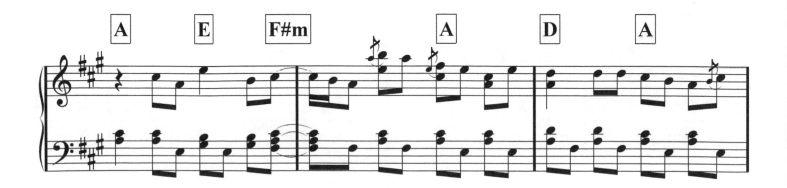

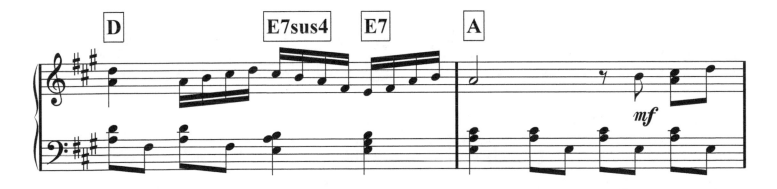

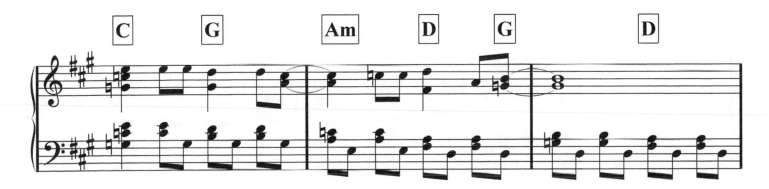

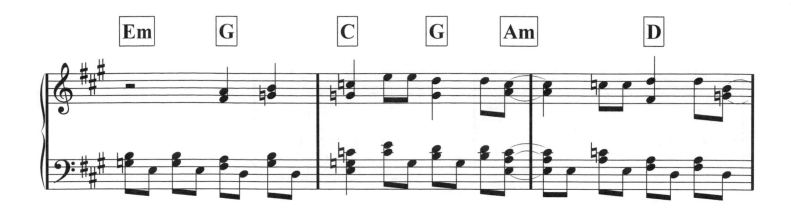

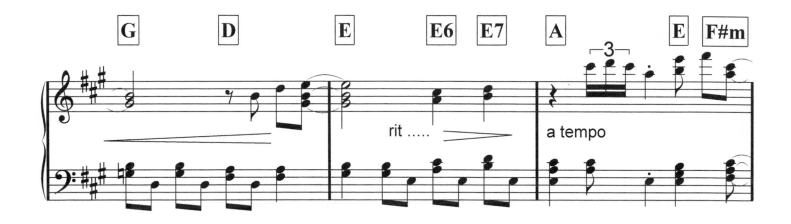

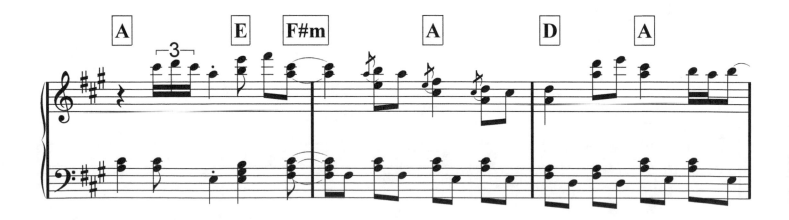

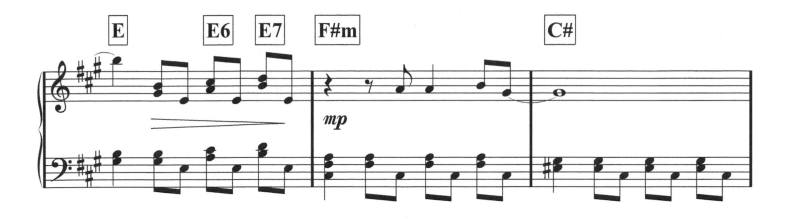

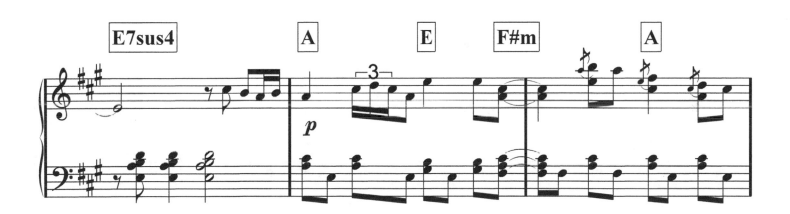

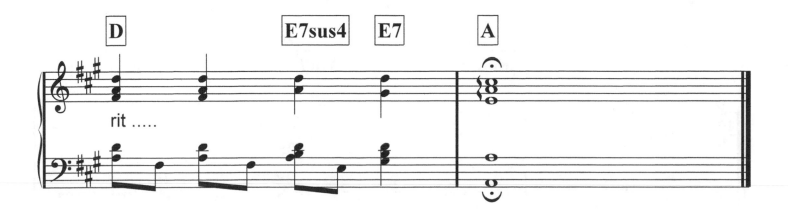

# "Light My Fire"
## The Doors

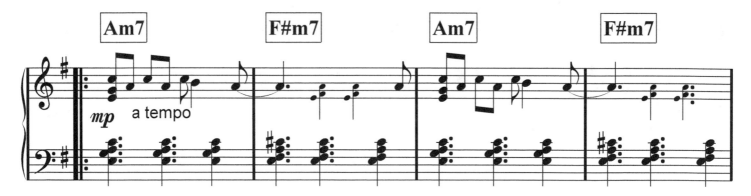

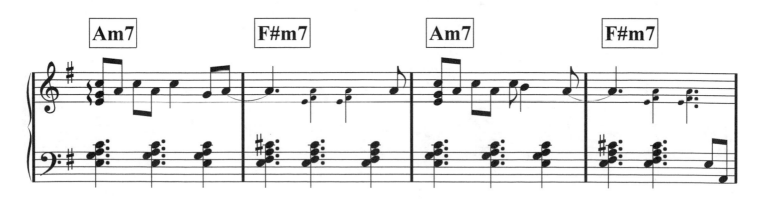

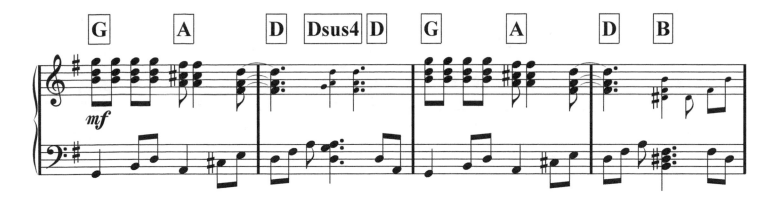

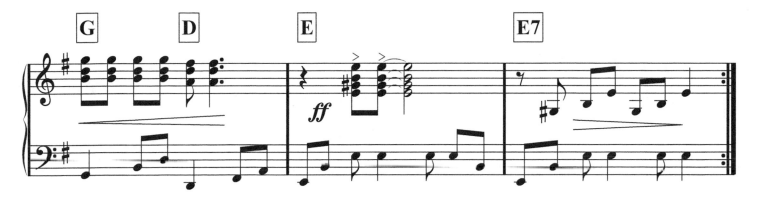

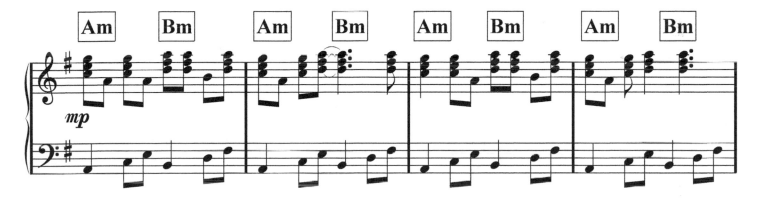

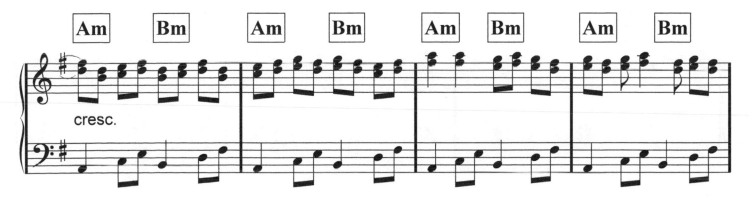

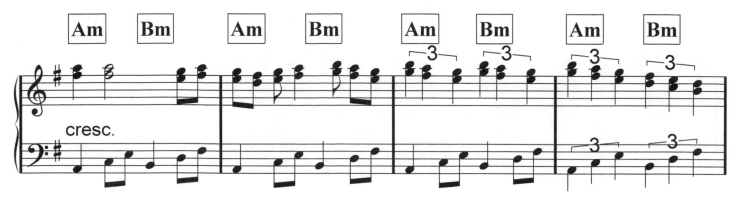

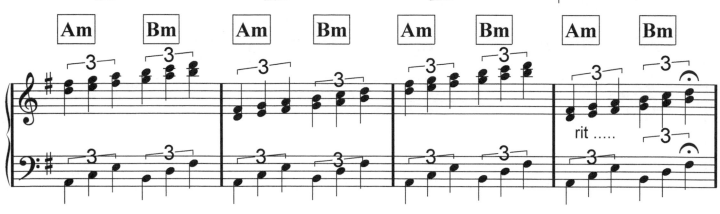

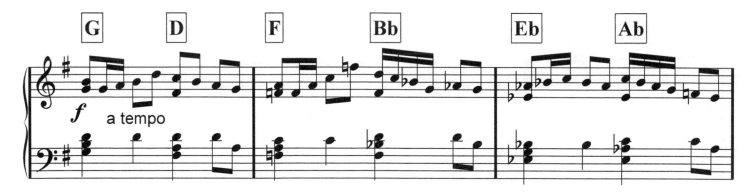

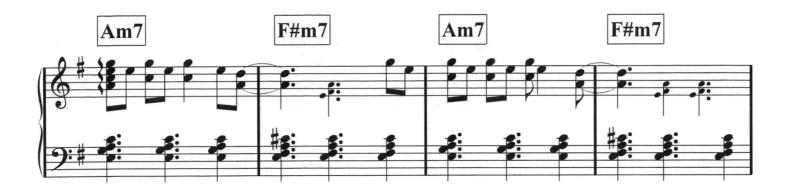

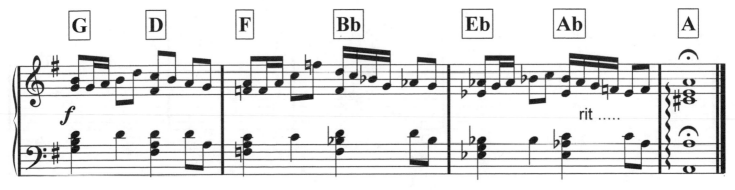

# "Life on Mars?"
## David Bowie

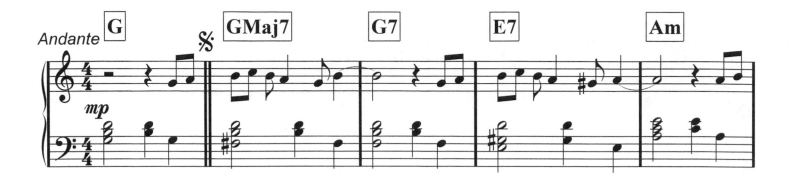

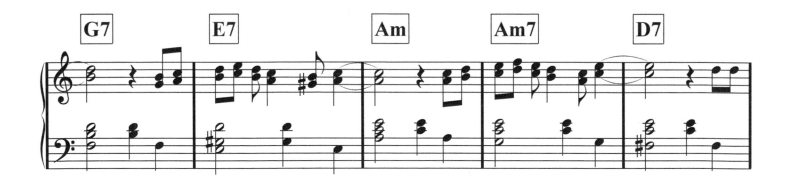

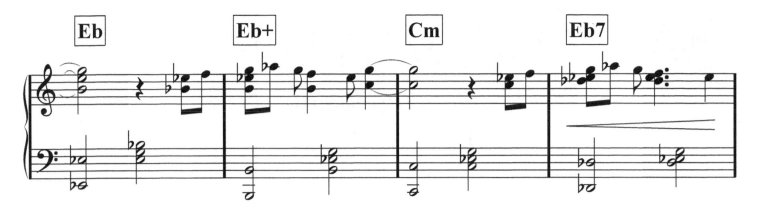

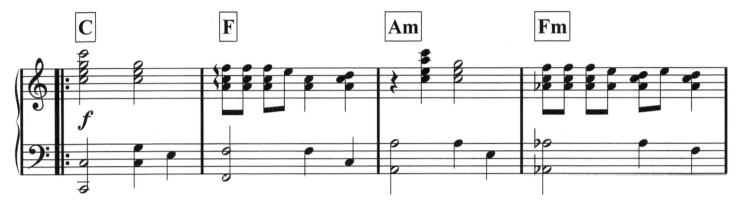

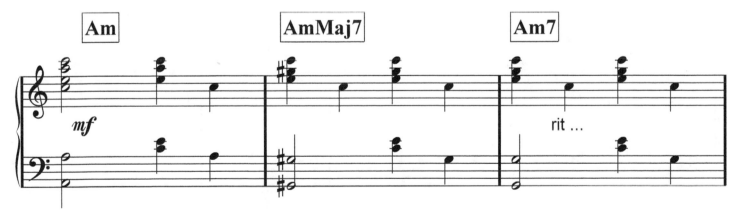

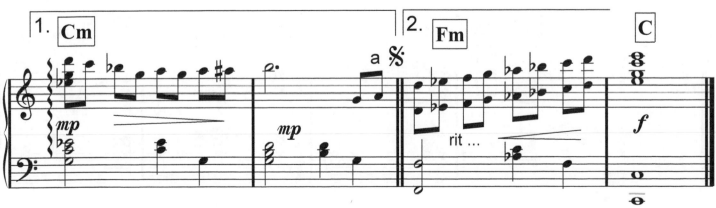

# "Going Home"
## (Theme from Local Hero)
### Dire Straits

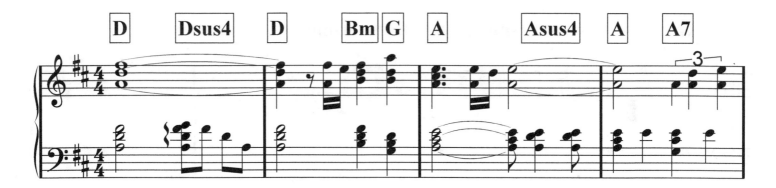

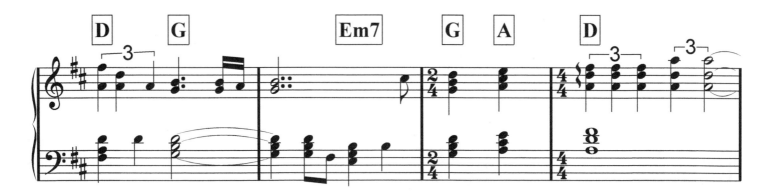

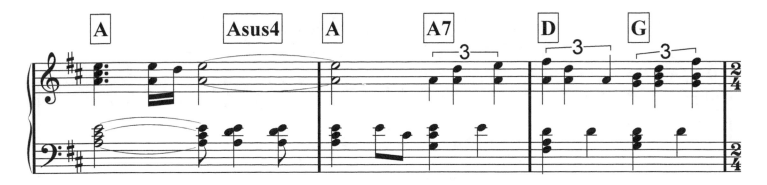

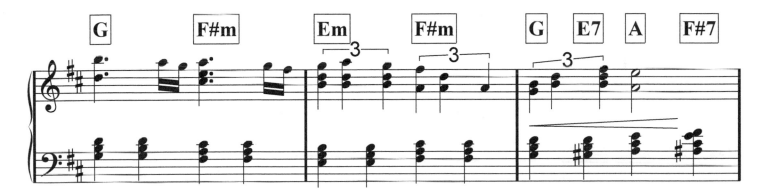

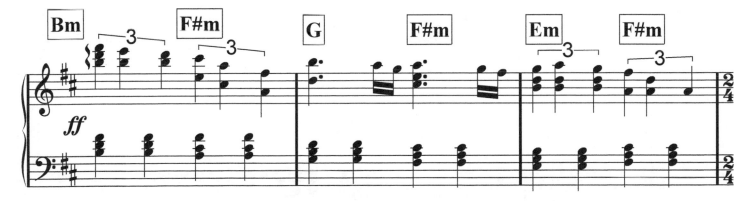

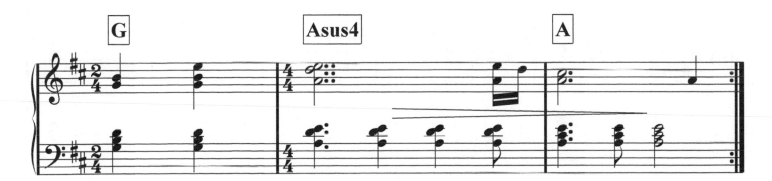

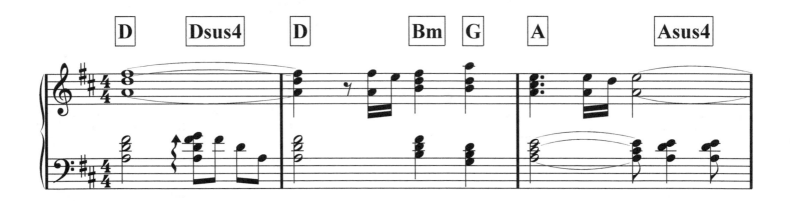

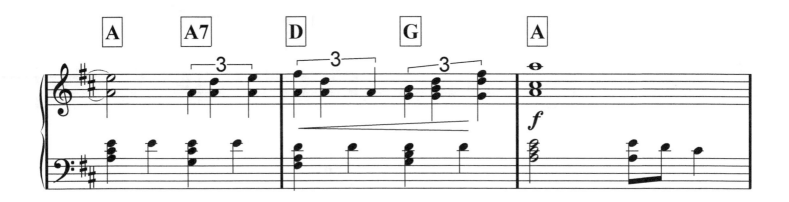

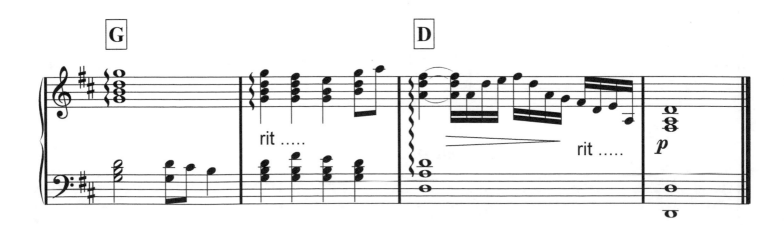

# "Something"
## The Beatles

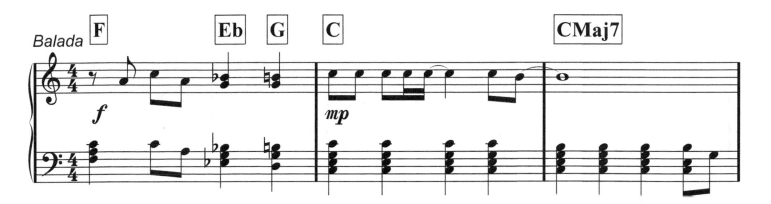

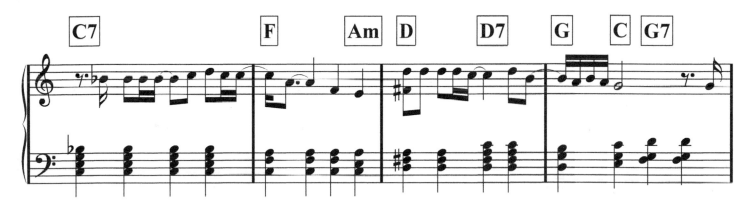

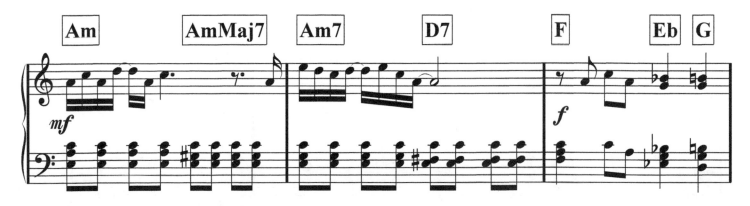

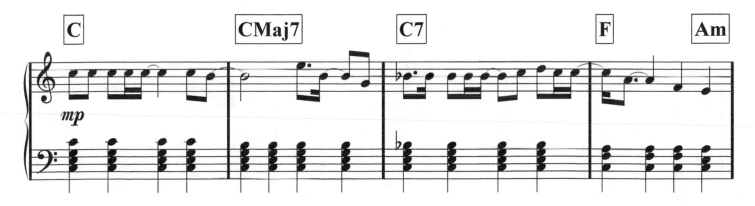

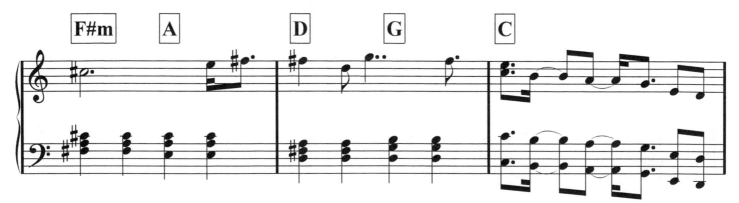

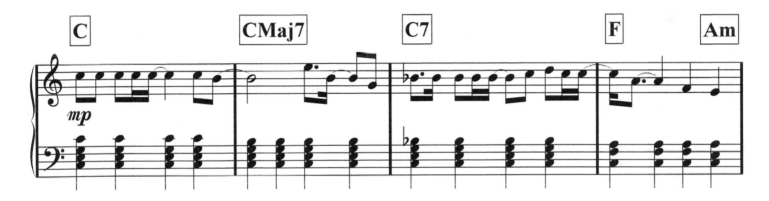

# "With or Without You"
## U2

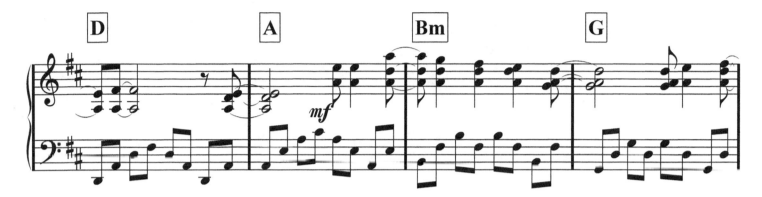

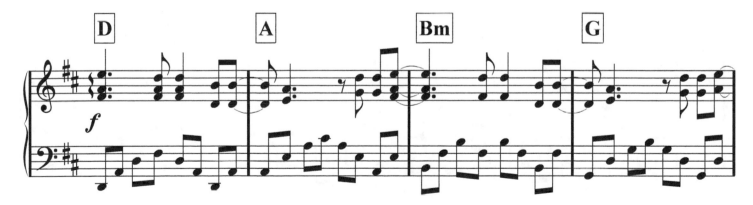

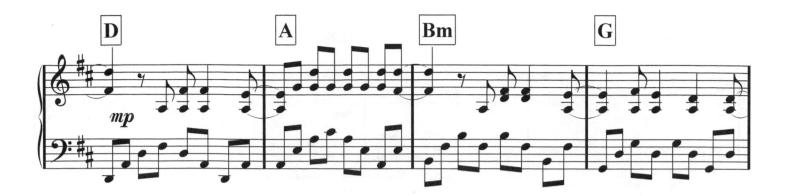

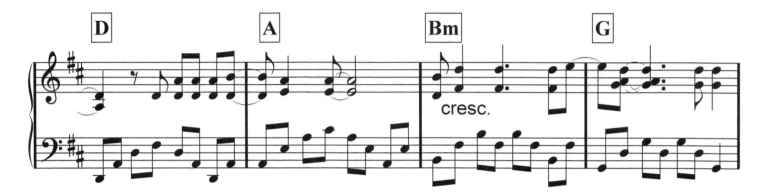

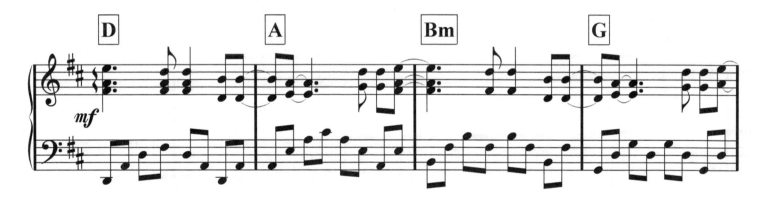

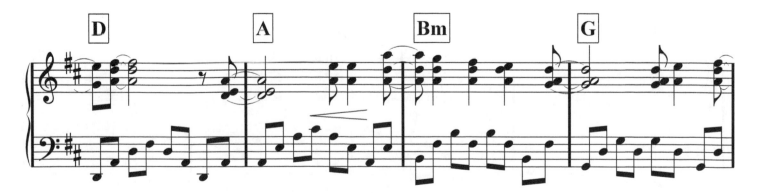

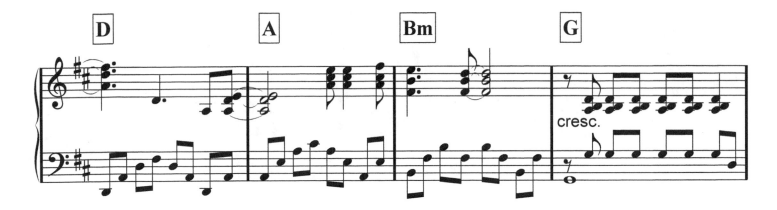

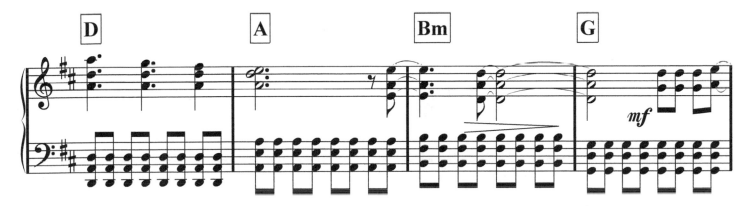

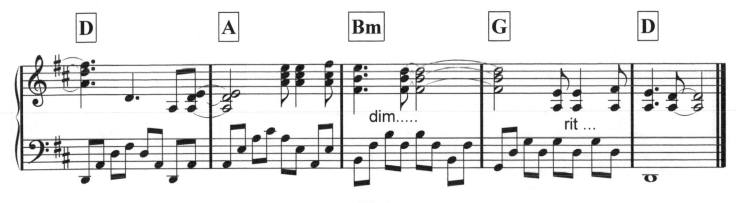

# "Bridge Over Troubled Water"
## Simon & Garfunkel

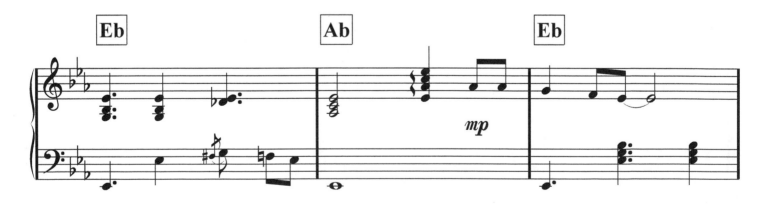

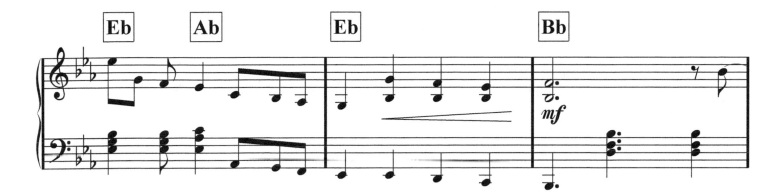

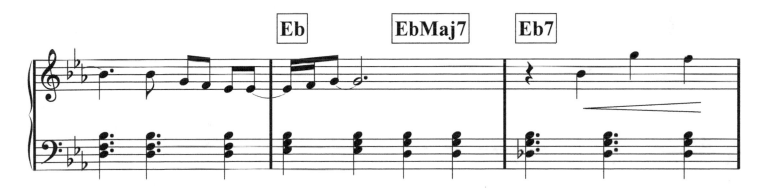

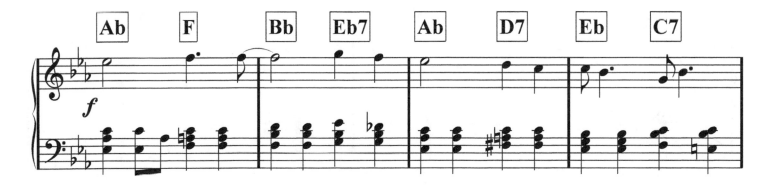

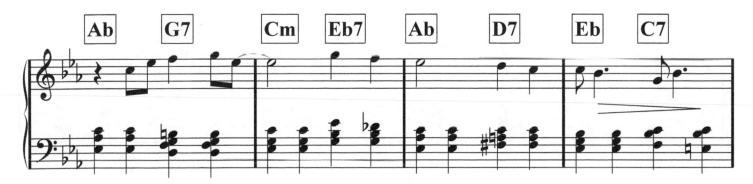

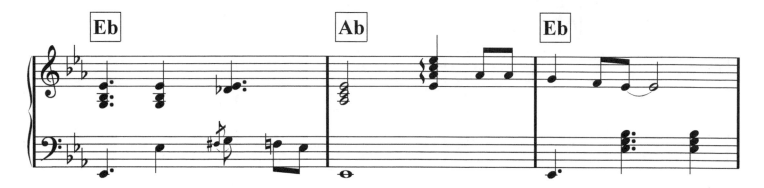

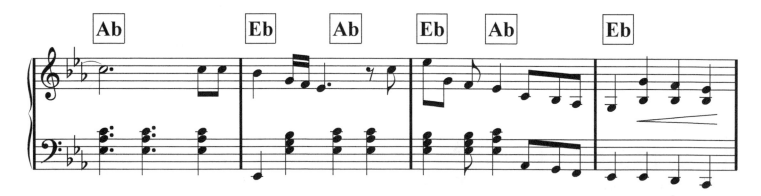

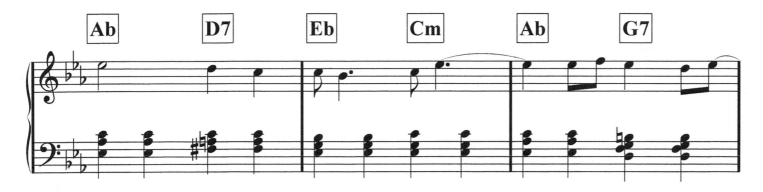

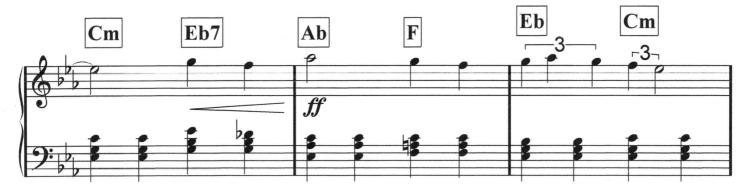

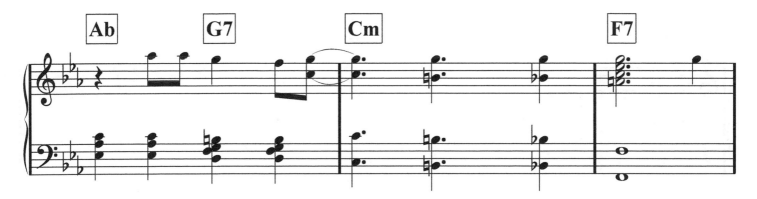

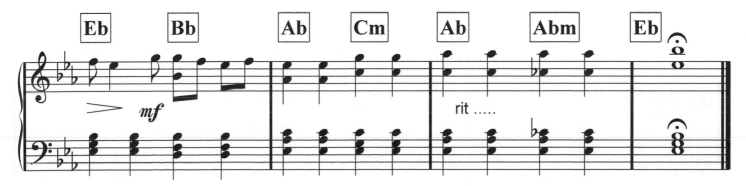

# "Morning Has Broken"
## Cat Stevens

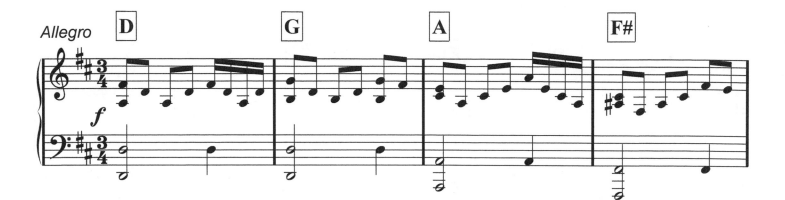

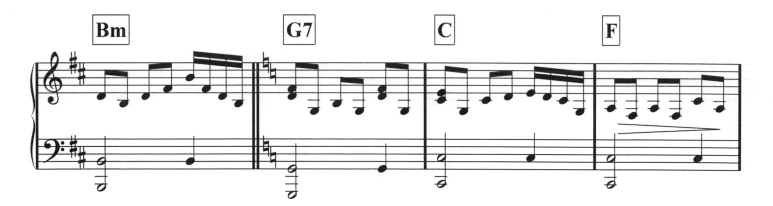

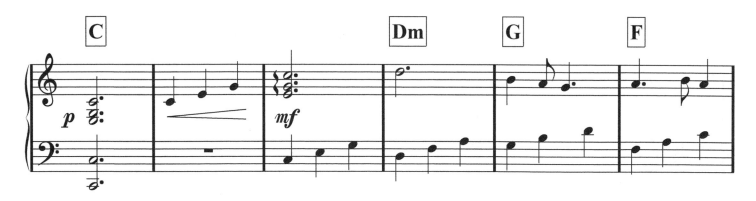

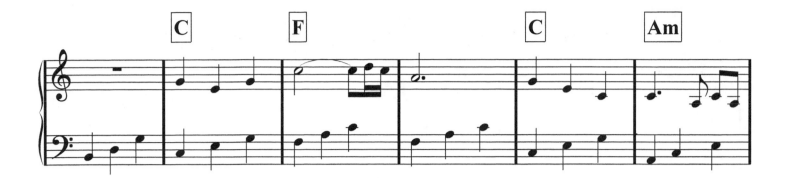

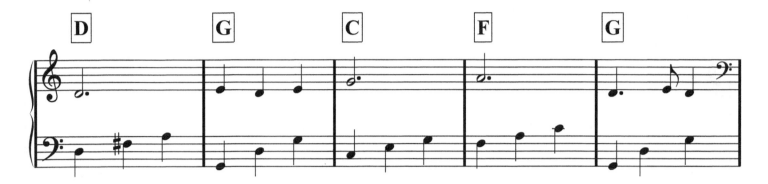

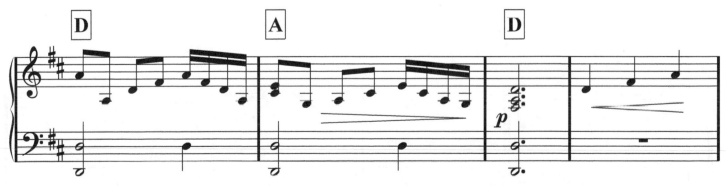

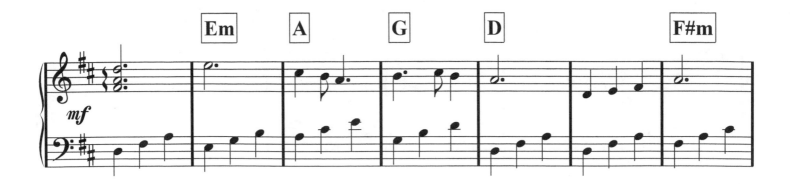

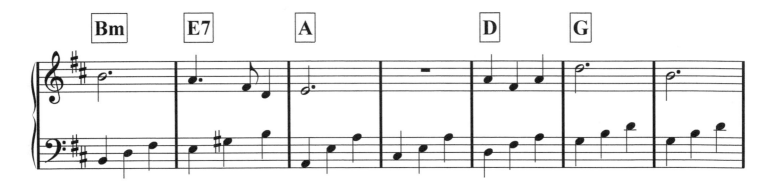

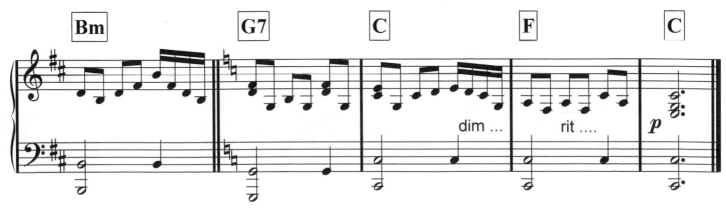

# "I Guess That's Why They Call It the Blues"

## Elton John

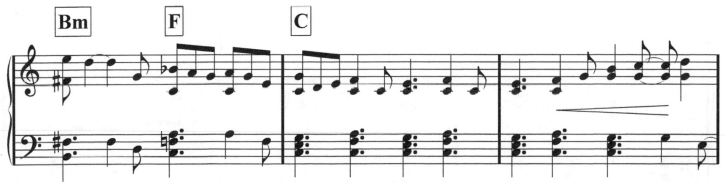

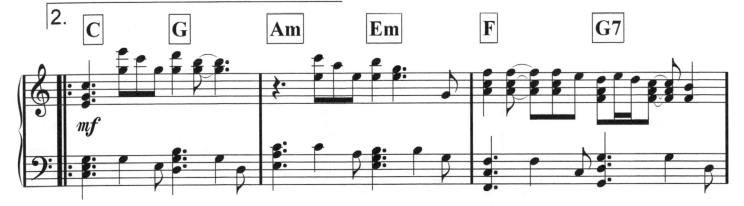

# "Summer of ´69"
## Bryan Adams

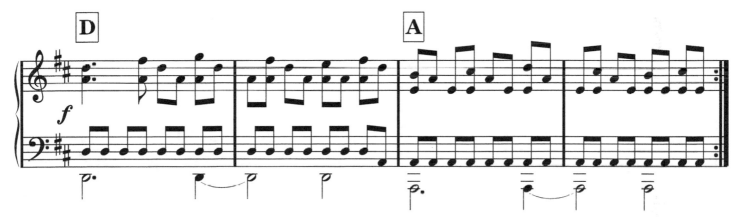

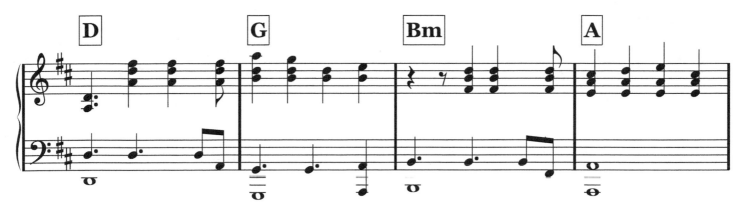

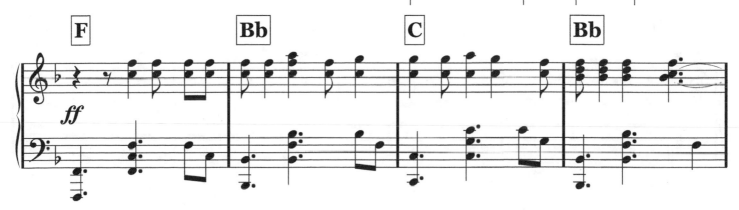

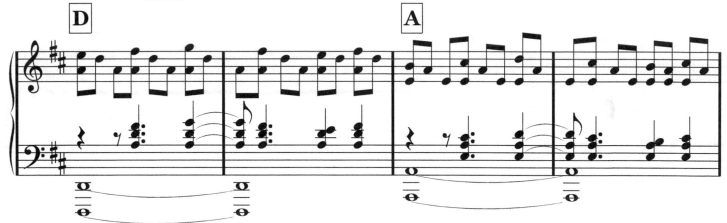

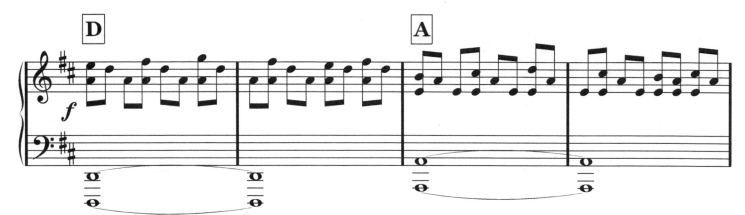

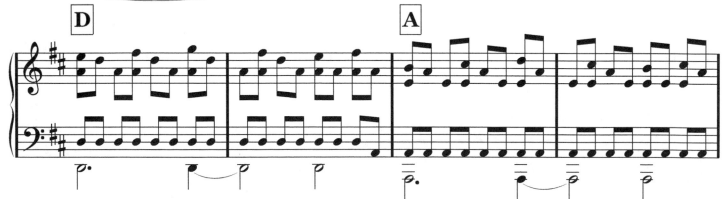

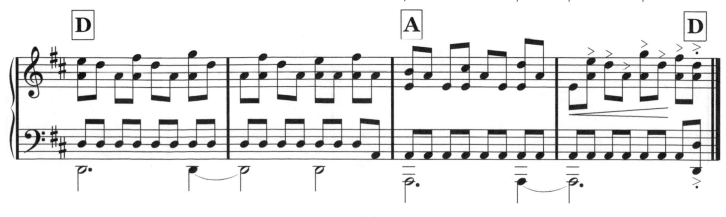

# "Message in a Bottle"
## The Police

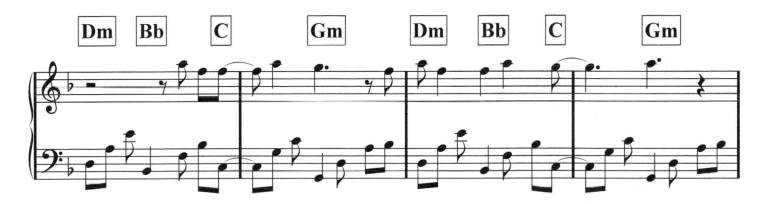

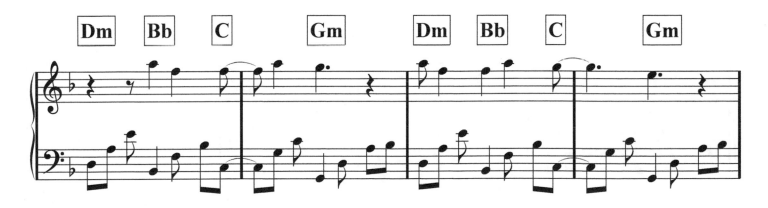

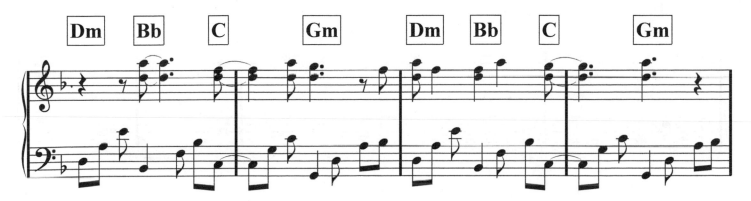

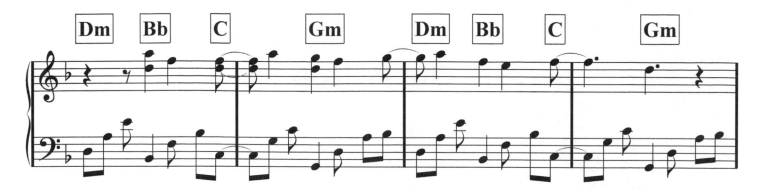

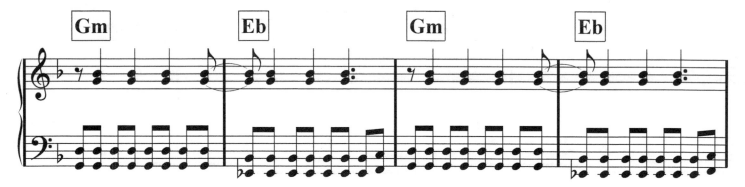

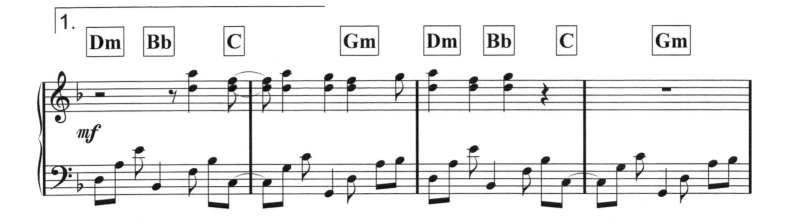

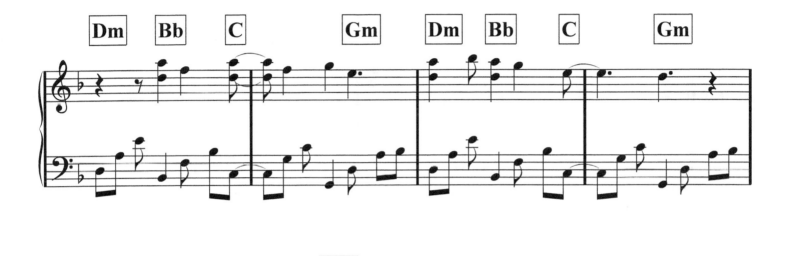

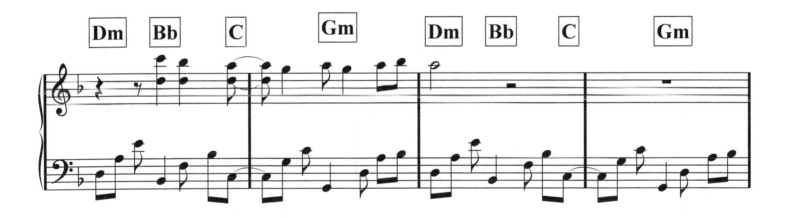

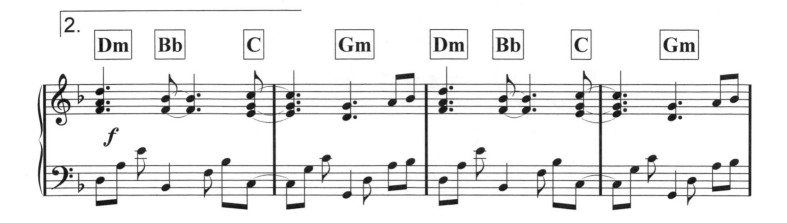

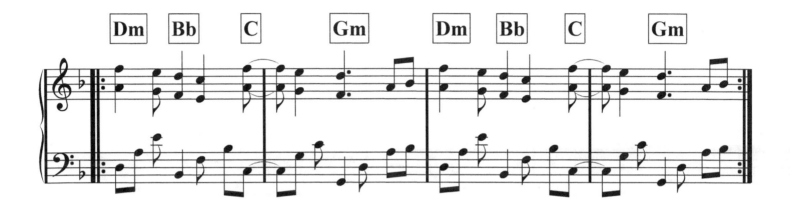

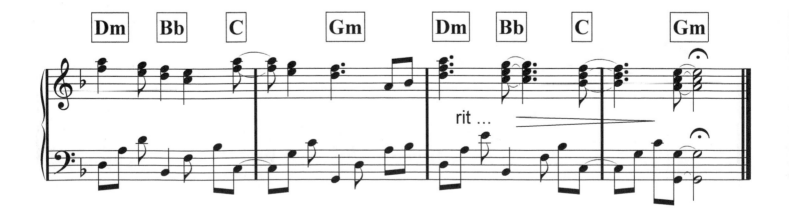

# "Desperado"
## Eagles

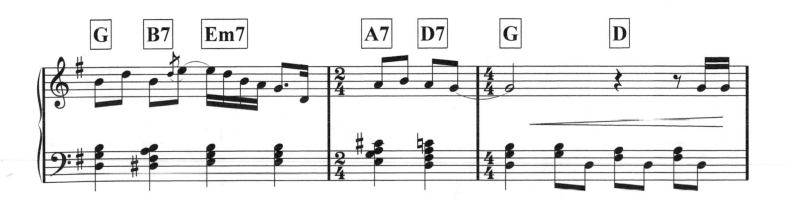

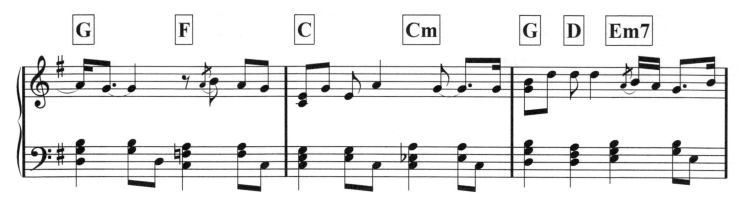

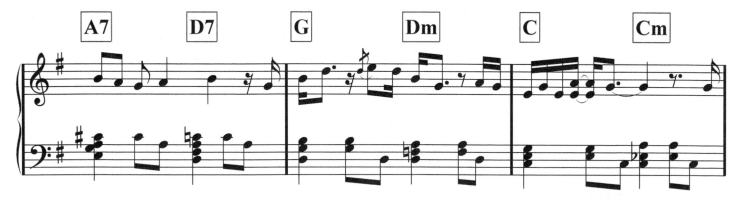

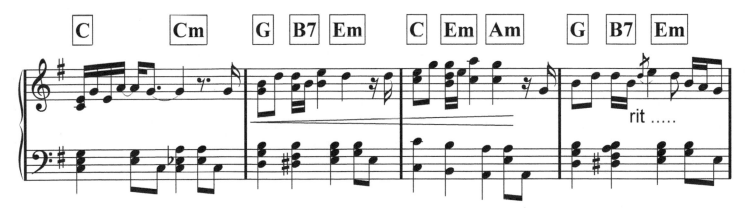

# "Just the Way You Are"
## Billy Joel

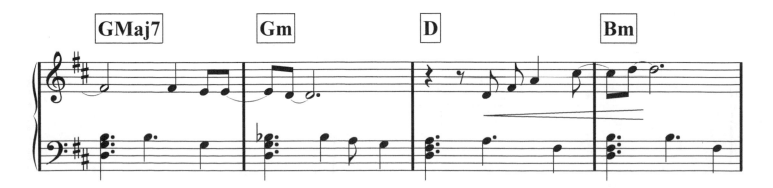

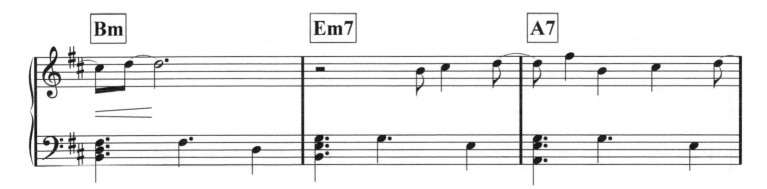

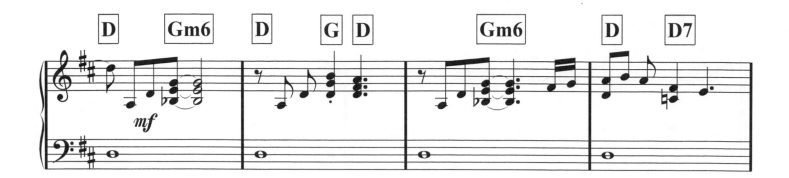

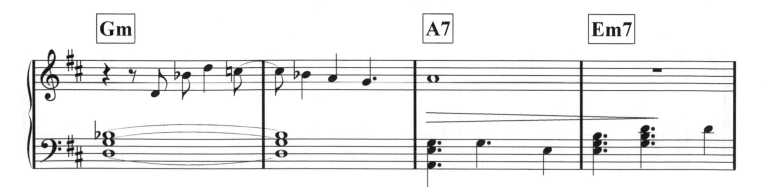

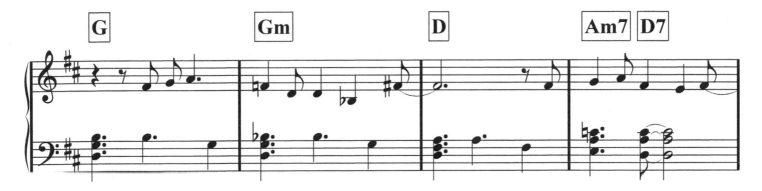

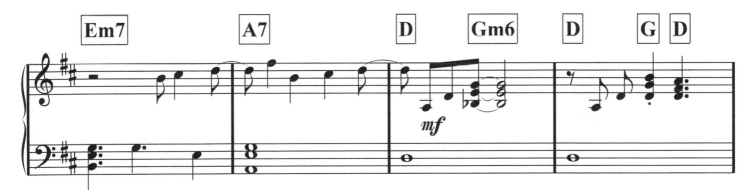

# "Kashmir"
## Led Zeppelin

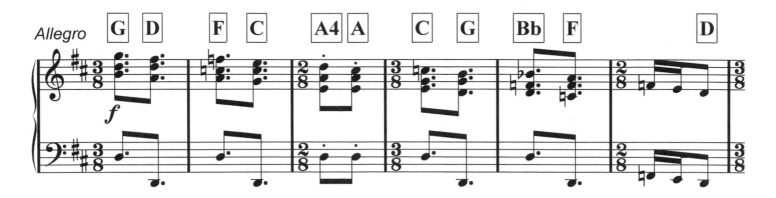

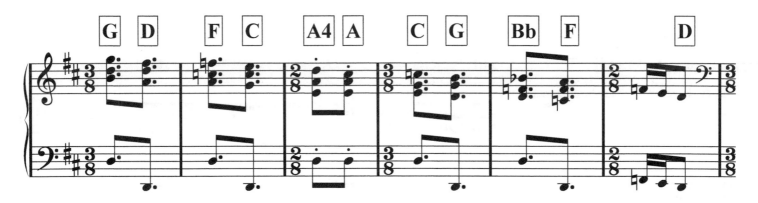

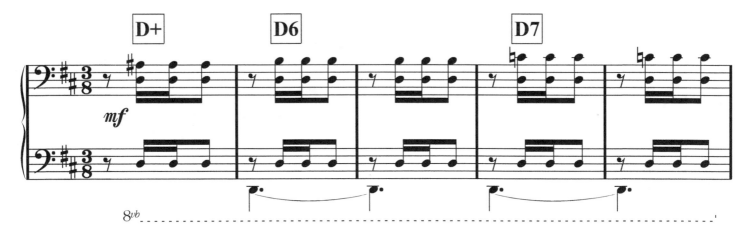

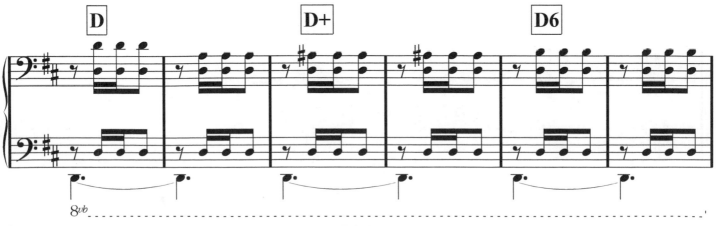

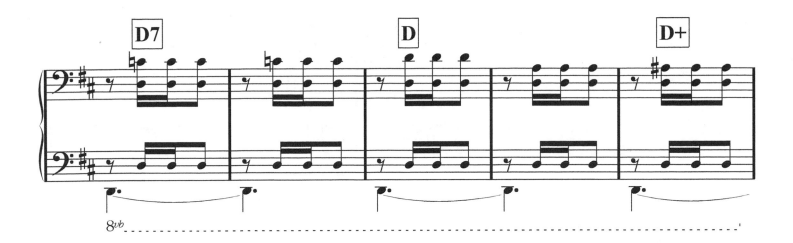

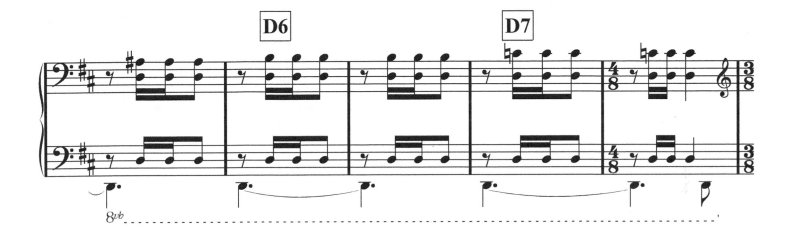

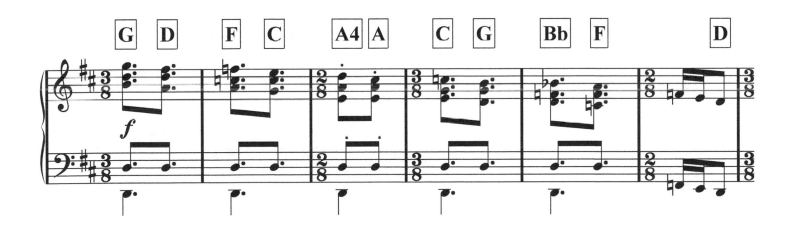

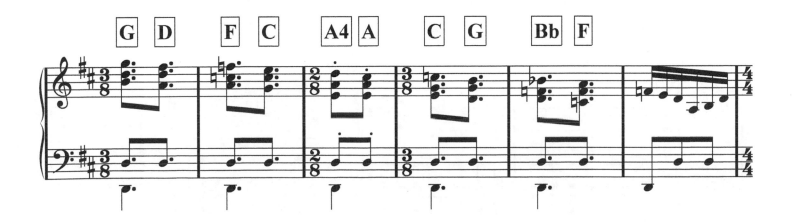

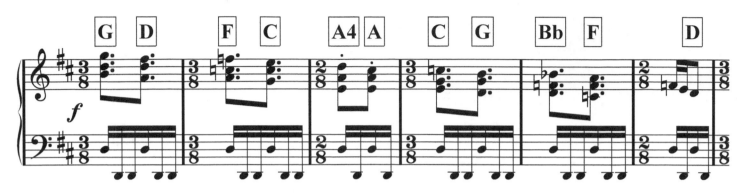

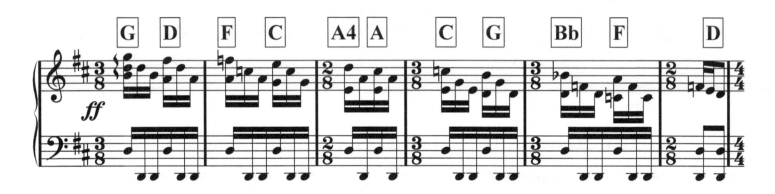

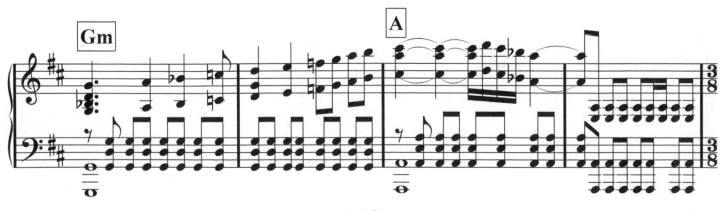

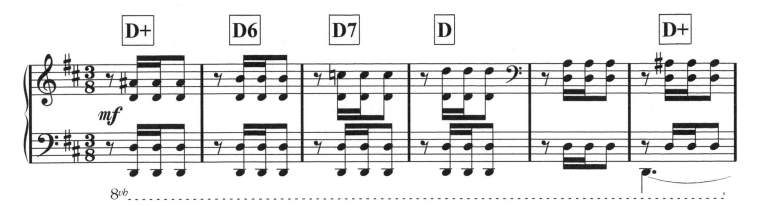

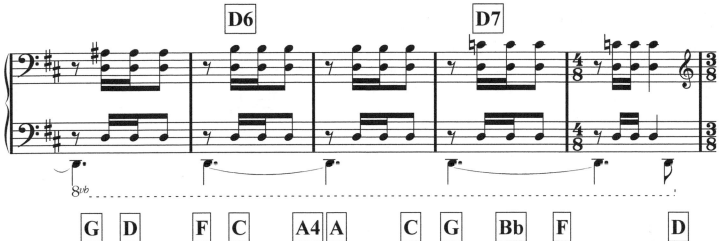

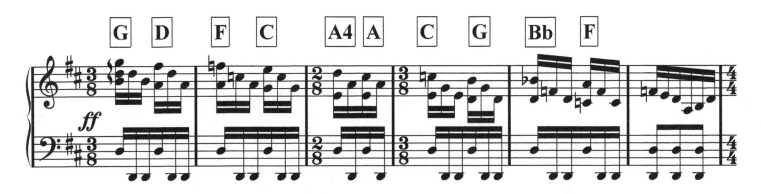

# "Bohemian Rhapsody"
## Queen

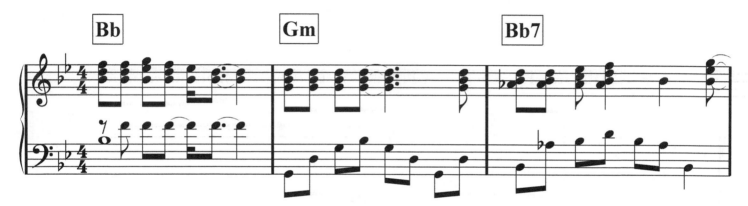

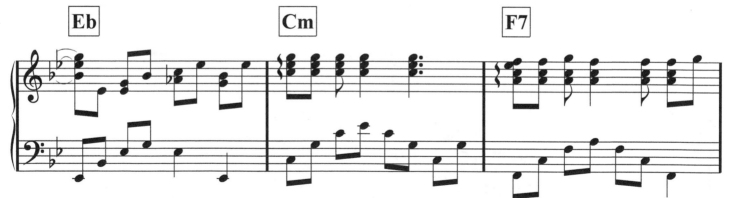

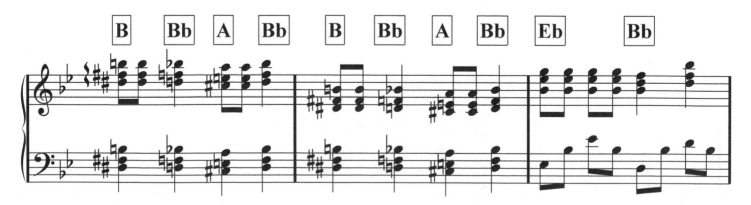

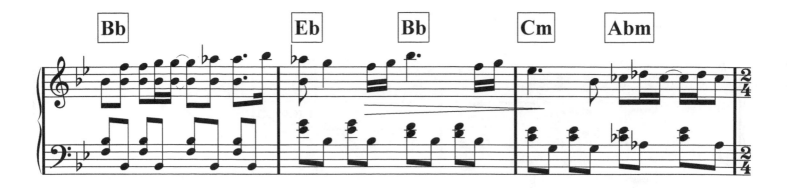

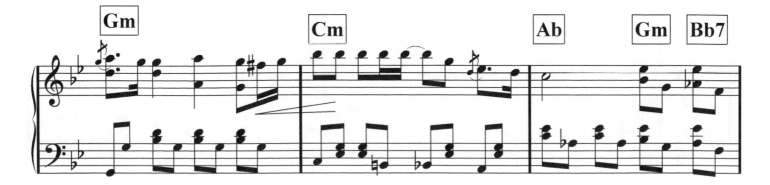

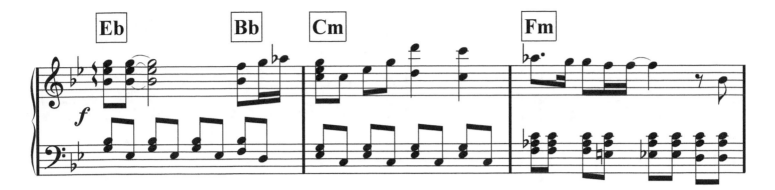

Vivace

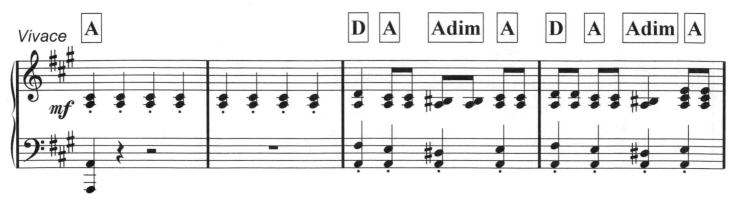

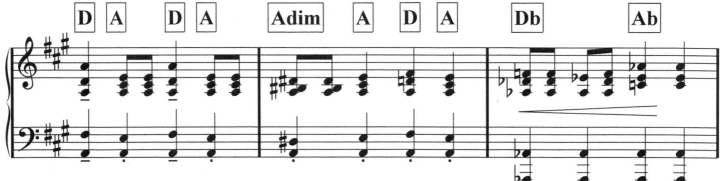

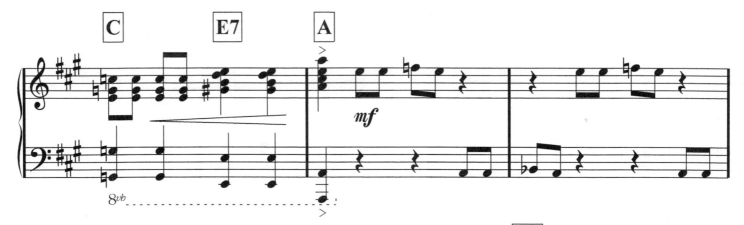

8vb

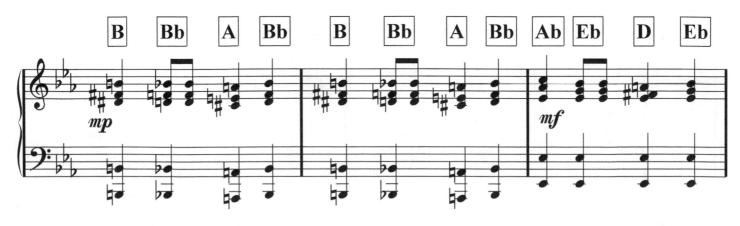

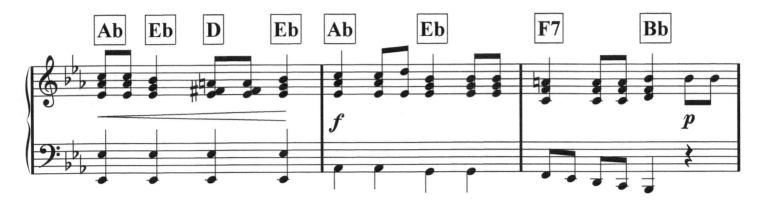

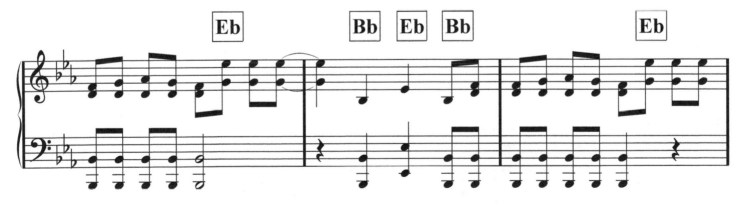

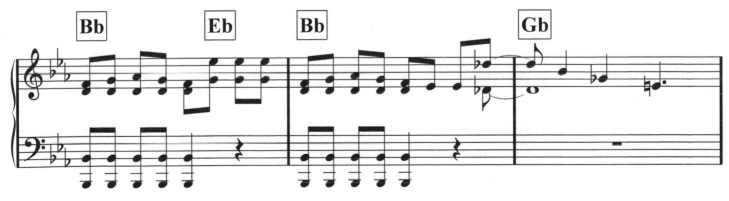

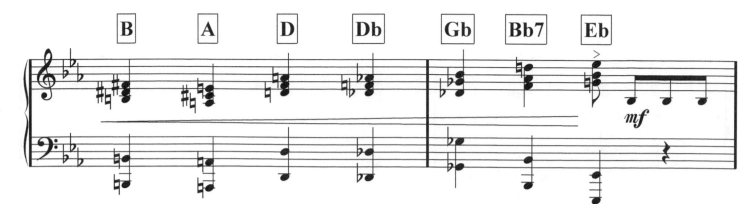

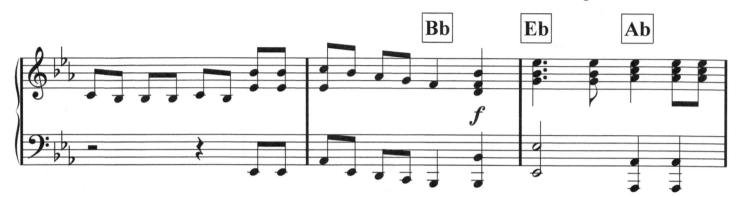

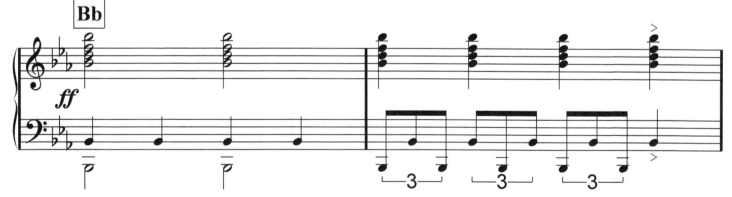

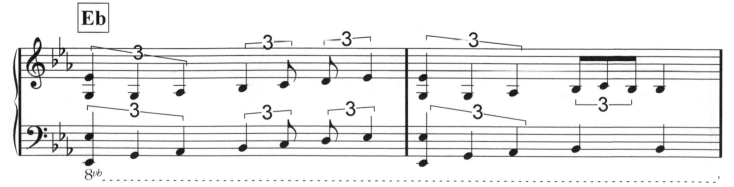

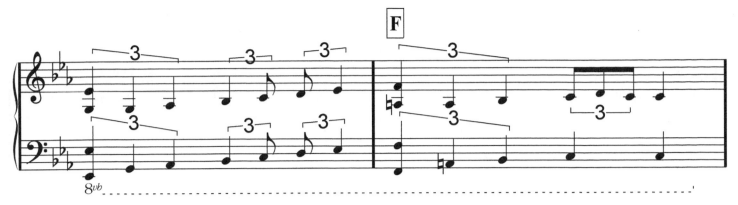

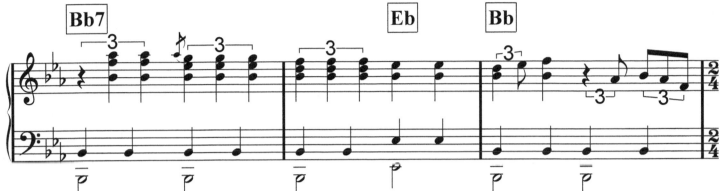

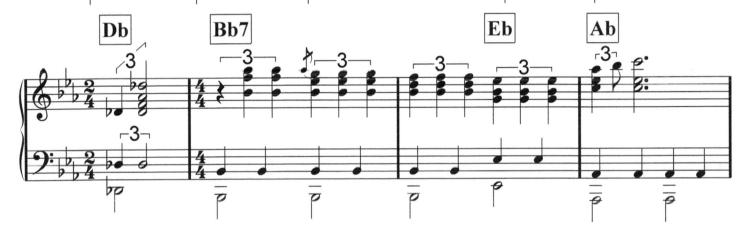

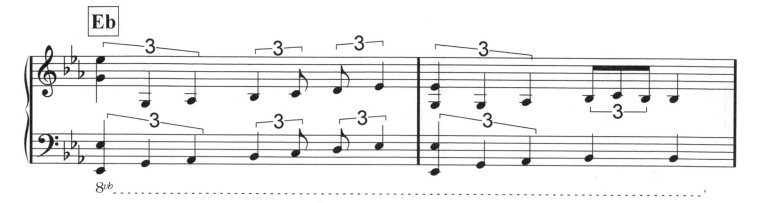

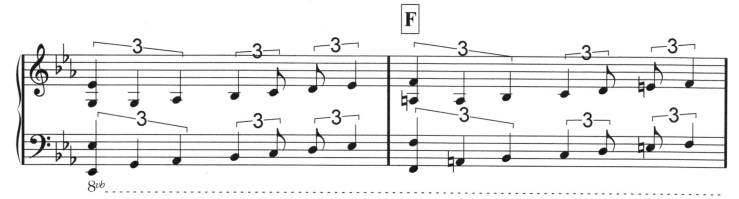

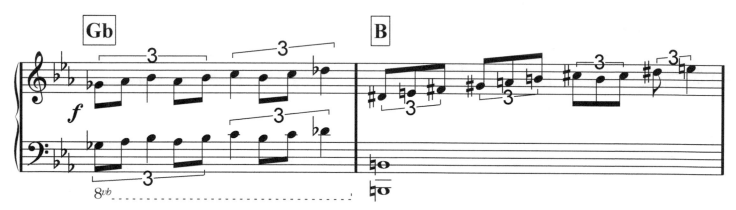

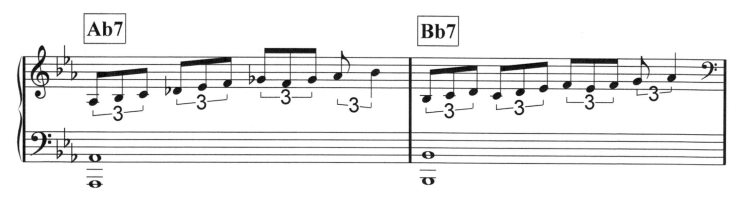

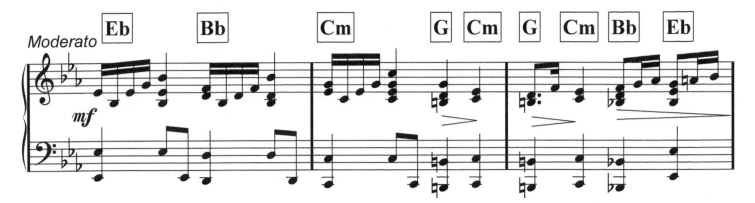

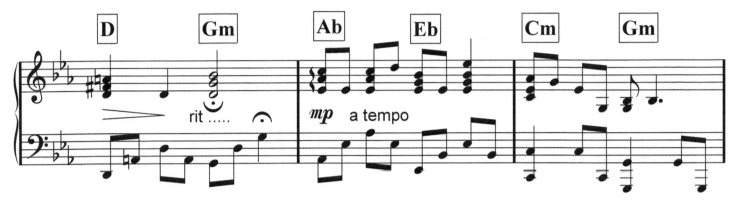

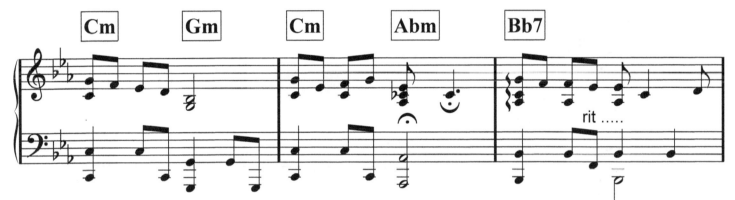

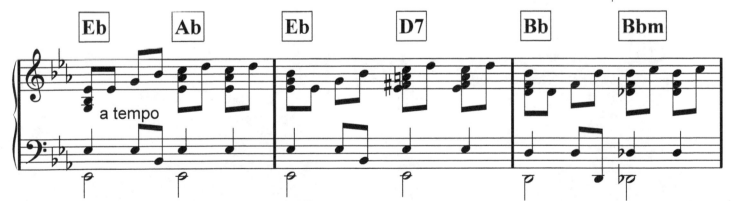